Grimm's Fairy Tales

Grimm's Fairy Tales

This edition published in 2019 by Sirius Publishing, a division of Arcturus Publishing Limited,
26/27 Bickels Yard, 151–153 Bermondsey Street,
London SE1 3HA

Copyright © Arcturus Holdings Limited

All rights reserved. No part of this publication may be reproduced, stored in a retrieval system, or transmitted, in any form or by any means, electronic, mechanical, photocopying, recording or otherwise, without prior written permission in accordance with the provisions of the Copyright Act 1956 (as amended). Any person or persons who do any unauthorised act in relation to this publication may be liable to criminal prosecution and civil claims for damages.

ISBN: 978-1-78950-397-5
AD005109UK

Printed in China

Contents

Introduction 7
The Frog-King, or Iron Henry 9
Cat and Mouse in Partnership 14
The Story of the Youth Who Went Forth to Learn
What Fear Was 18
The Wonderful Musician 30
The Twelve Brothers 34
Rapunzel 40
The Three Spinners 45
Hansel and Grethel 48
The Valiant Little Tailor 57
Cinderella 67
The Mouse, the Bird and the Sausage 76
Little Red-Cap 78
The Bremen Town-Musicians 83
The Singing Bone 87
The Devil with the Three Golden Hairs 90
The Elves 98
The Robber Bridegroom 102
Old Sultan 107
The Six Swans 110
Briar-Rose 116
Little Snow-White 121

Rumpelstiltskin	132
The Golden Goose	136
Jorinda and Joringel	140
The Old Man and His Grandson	144
The Goose-Girl	145
The King of the Golden Mountain	153
The Peasant's Wise Daughter	161
The Devil's Sooty Brother	166
Bearskin	170
The Three Army Surgeons	176
The Seven Swabians	180
The Devil and His Grandmother	184
The Iron Stove	188
The Lazy Spinner	195
The Four Skilful Brothers	198
The Lambkin and the Little Fish	204
The Old Man Made Young Again	207
Snow-White and Rose-Red	209
The Duration of Life	217
Death's Messengers	219
The Hare and the Hedgehog	221
The Crystal Ball	226
The Boots of Buffalo-Leather	230
The Golden Key	235

INTRODUCTION

Fairy tales show us things that have never been – witches, dragons, dwarves spinning straw into gold. But they also show us things that still are – orphans, poverty and hunger.

In 1812, when Jacob and Wilhelm Grimm published *Children's and Household* Tales (the original title of what we nowadays know as *Grimm's Fairy Tales*), they were struggling to support themselves and their three siblings, and eating only one meal a day. The unexpected death of their father when they were boys had brought immediate financial crisis. Their aunt arranged their education, but their poverty set them apart. To escape their loneliness, they studied hard, both at school and later at university.

There, they embraced the intellectual fashions surrounding them, including a romantic belief in the value of folk tales, and the fear that these were under threat. For centuries, housewives had told stories to relieve the tedium of domestic chores such as spinning. Now machines were taking over. Would the housewives' stories be forgotten?

No, insisted the brothers; hence their collection of *Children's and Household Tales.*

Few readers noticed. The *Tales* were heavy with footnotes, and sales were poor. Further volumes followed, and always the scholarship was impressive – the brothers noted the influence of Germanic and Norse mythology; pointed out variants in other cultures, from Ireland to Japan; and demonstrated that the same story could vary between regions, as shown in 'The Twelve Brothers' and 'The Seven Swans'.

But still they enjoyed no commercial success. It came at last, in 1825, with the publication of a *Small Edition*, fifty tales rewritten by Wilhelm for young readers. Footnotes disappeared, illustrations were added, and the violence was tempered – no longer were children cannibalized, but step-mothers could still be burnt!

If we are troubled today by these evil step-mothers, it's worth noticing that the tales hardly endorse patriarchy. Kings plan to murder their sons; her own father calls Cinderella a 'stunted kitchen-wench'. In the world of the tales, it is power, not gender, that enables evil.

But we should probably not search too hard for moral instruction. For more than three decades, the brothers revised and reworked their stories to cater for changing tastes. And even after their deaths the stories evolved. It was later audiences who insisted that Sleeping Beauty's prince must be valiant, and that Cinderella's step-sisters could not use knives. It was the Nazis who discovered in them solid Aryan principles – and W. H. Auden who discovered an essential part of Western culture, 'next to the Bible in importance'.

These tales, which in this edition are based on the original English translation by Margaret Hunt from 1884, are whatever we want them to be.

So, settle down, and begin.

THE FROG-KING, OR IRON HENRY

In old times when wishing still helped one, there lived a king whose daughters were all beautiful, but the youngest was so beautiful that the sun itself, which has seen so much, was astonished whenever it shone in her face. Close by the King's castle lay a great dark forest, and under an old lime-tree in the forest was a well, and when the day was very warm, the King's child went out into the forest and sat down by the side of the cool fountain, and when she was dull she took a golden ball, and threw it up on high and caught it, and this ball was her favourite plaything.

Now it so happened that on one occasion the princess's golden ball did not fall into the little hand which she was holding up for it, but on to the ground beyond, and rolled straight into the water. The King's daughter followed it with her eyes, but it vanished, and the well was deep, so deep that the bottom could not be seen. On this she began to cry, and cried louder and louder, and could not be comforted. And as she thus lamented someone said to her, 'What ails thee, King's daughter? Thou weepest so that even a stone would show pity.' She looked round to the side from whence the voice came, and saw a frog stretching forth its thick, ugly head from the water. 'Ah! old water-splasher, is it thou?' said she; 'I am weeping for my golden ball, which has fallen into the well.'

'Be quiet, and do not weep,' answered the frog, 'I can help thee, but what wilt thou give me if I bring thy plaything up again?'

'Whatever thou wilt have, dear frog,' said she. 'My clothes, my pearls and jewels, and even the golden crown which I am wearing.'

The frog answered, 'I do not care for thy clothes, thy pearls and jewels, or thy golden crown, but if thou wilt love me and let me be thy companion and play-fellow, and sit by thee at thy little table, and eat off thy little golden plate, and drink out of thy little cup, and sleep in thy little bed – if thou wilt promise me this I will go down below, and bring thee thy golden ball up again.'

'Oh yes,' said she, 'I promise thee all thou wishest, if thou wilt but bring me my ball back again.' She, however, thought, 'How the silly frog does talk! He lives in the water with the other frogs, and croaks, and can be no companion to any human being!'

But the frog when he had received this promise, put his head into the water and sank down, and in a short while came swimming up again with the ball in his mouth, and threw it on the grass. The King's daughter was delighted to see her pretty plaything once more, and picked it up, and ran away with it. 'Wait, wait,' said the frog. 'Take me with thee. I can't run as thou canst.' But what did it avail him to scream his croak, croak, after her, as loudly as he could? She did not listen to it, but ran home and soon forgot the poor frog, who was forced to go back into his well again.

The next day when she had seated herself at table with the King and all the courtiers, and was eating from her little golden plate, something came creeping splish splash, splish splash, up the marble staircase, and when it had got to the top, it knocked at the door and cried, 'Princess, youngest princess, open the door for me.' She ran to see who was outside, but when she opened the door, there sat the frog in front of it. Then she slammed the door to, in great haste, sat down to dinner again, and was quite frightened. The King saw plainly that her heart was beating violently, and said, 'My child, what art thou so afraid of? Is there perchance a giant outside who wants to carry thee away?'

'Ah, no,' replied she. 'It is no giant but a disgusting frog.'

'What does a frog want with thee?'

'Ah, dear father, yesterday as I was in the forest sitting by the well, playing, my golden ball fell into the water. And because I cried so, the frog brought it out again for me, and because he so insisted, I promised him he should be my companion, but I never thought he would be able to come out of his water! And now he is outside there, and wants to come in to me.'

In the meantime it knocked a second time, and cried,

'Princess! youngest princess!
Open the door for me!
Dost thou not know what thou saidst to me
Yesterday by the cool waters of the fountain?
Princess, youngest princess!
Open the door for me!'

Then said the King, 'That which thou hast promised must thou perform. Go and let him in.'

She went and opened the door, and the frog hopped in and followed her, step by step, to her chair. There he sat still and cried, 'Lift me up beside thee.' She delayed, until at last the King commanded her to do it. When the frog was once on the chair he wanted to be on the table, and when he was on the table he said, 'Now, push thy little golden plate nearer to me that we may eat together.' She did this, but it was easy to see that she did not do it willingly. The frog enjoyed what he ate, but almost every mouthful she took choked her. At length, he said, 'I have eaten and am satisfied; now I am tired, carry me into thy little room and make thy little silken bed ready, and we will both lie down and go to sleep.'

The King's daughter began to cry, for she was afraid of the cold frog which she did not like to touch, and which was now to sleep in her pretty, clean little bed. But the King grew angry and said, 'He who helped thee when thou wert in trouble ought not afterwards to be despised by thee.'

So she took hold of the frog with two fingers, carried him upstairs, and put him in a corner. But when she was in bed he crept to her and said, 'I am tired, I want to sleep as well as thou, lift me up or I will tell thy father.' Then she was terribly angry, and took him up and threw him with all her might against the wall. 'Now, thou wilt be quiet, odious frog,' said she.

But when he fell down he was no frog but a King's son with beautiful kind eyes. He by her father's will was now her dear companion and husband. Then he told her how he had been bewitched by a wicked witch, and how no one could have delivered him from the well but herself, and that tomorrow they would go together into his kingdom. Then they went to sleep, and next morning when the sun awoke them, a carriage came driving up with eight white horses, which had white ostrich feathers on their heads, and were harnessed with golden chains, and behind stood the young King's servant Faithful Henry. Faithful Henry had been so unhappy when his master was changed into a frog, that he had caused three iron bands to be laid round his heart, lest it should burst with grief and sadness. The carriage was to conduct the young King into his Kingdom. Faithful Henry helped them both in, and placed himself behind again, and was full of joy because of this deliverance. And when they had driven a part of the way, the King's son heard a cracking behind him as if something had broken. So he turned round and cried, 'Henry, the carriage is breaking.'

'No, master, it is not the carriage. It is a band from my heart, which was put there in my great pain when you were a frog and imprisoned in the well.'

Again and once again while they were on their way something cracked, and each time the King's son thought the carriage was breaking; but it was only the bands which were springing from the heart of Faithful Henry because his master was set free and was happy.

CAT AND MOUSE IN PARTNERSHIP

A certain cat had made the acquaintance of a mouse, and had said so much to her about the great love and friendship she felt for her, that at length the mouse agreed that they should live and keep house together. 'But we must make a provision for winter, or else we shall suffer from hunger,' said the cat, 'and you, little mouse, cannot venture everywhere, or you will be caught in a trap some day.'

The good advice was followed, and a pot of fat was bought, but they did not know where to put it. At length, after much consideration, the cat said, 'I know no place where it will be better stored up than in the church, for no one dares take anything away from there. We will set it beneath the altar, and not touch it until we are really in need of it.' So the pot was placed in safety, but it was not long before the cat had a great yearning for it, and said to the mouse, 'I want to tell you something, little mouse; my cousin has brought a little son into the world, and has asked me to be godmother; he is white with brown spots, and I am to hold him over the font at the christening. Let me go out today, and you look after the house by yourself.'

'Yes, yes,' answered the mouse, 'by all means go, and if you get anything very good, think of me, I should like a drop of sweet red christening wine too.'

All this, however, was untrue; the cat had no cousin, and had not been asked to be godmother. She went straight to the church, stole to the pot of fat, began to lick at it, and licked the top of the fat off. Then she took a walk upon the roofs of the town, looked out for opportunities, and then stretched herself in the sun, and licked her lips whenever she thought of the pot of fat, and not until it was evening did she return home.

'Well, here you are again,' said the mouse, 'no doubt you have had a merry day.'

'All went off well,' answered the cat.

'What name did they give the child?'

'Top off!' said the cat quite coolly.

'Top off!' cried the mouse, 'that is a very odd and uncommon name, is it a usual one in your family?'

'What does it signify,' said the cat, 'it is no worse than Crumb-stealer, as your god-children are called.'

Before long the cat was seized by another fit of longing. She said to the mouse, 'You must do me a favour, and once more manage the house for a day alone. I am again asked to be godmother, and, as the child has a white ring round its neck, I cannot refuse.'

The good mouse consented, but the cat crept behind the town walls to the church, and devoured half the pot of fat. 'Nothing ever seems so good as what one keeps to oneself,' said she, and was quite satisfied with her day's work.

When she went home the mouse inquired, 'And what was this child christened?'

'Half-done,' answered the cat.

'Half-done! What are you saying? I never heard the name in my life, I'll wager anything it is not in the calendar!'

The cat's mouth soon began to water for some more licking. 'All good things go in threes,' said she, 'I am asked to stand godmother again. The child is quite black, only it has white paws, but with that exception, it has not a single white hair on its whole body; this only happens once every few years, you will let me go, won't you?'

'Top-off! Half-done!' answered the mouse, 'they are such odd names, they make me very thoughtful.'

'You sit at home,' said the cat, 'in your dark-grey fur coat and long tail, and are filled with fancies. That's because you do not go out in the daytime.'

During the cat's absence the mouse cleaned the house, and put it in order but the greedy cat entirely emptied the pot of fat. 'When everything is eaten up one has some peace,' said she to herself, and well filled and fat she did not return home till night. The mouse at once asked what name had been given to the third child. 'It will not please you more than the others,' said the cat. 'He is called All-gone.'

'All-gone,' cried the mouse, 'that is the most suspicious name of all! I have never seen it in print. All-gone; what can that mean?' and she shook her head, curled herself up, and lay down to sleep.

From this time forth no one invited the cat to be godmother, but when the winter had come and there was no longer anything to be found outside, the mouse thought of their provision, and said, 'Come cat, we will go to our pot of fat which we have stored up for ourselves – we shall enjoy that.'

'Yes,' answered the cat, 'you will enjoy it as much as you would enjoy sticking that dainty tongue of yours out of the window.'

They set out on their way, but when they arrived, the pot of fat certainly was still in its place, but it was empty. 'Alas!' said the mouse, 'now I see what has happened, now it comes to light! You are a true friend! You have devoured all when you were standing godmother. First top off, then half done, then—.'

'Will you hold your tongue,' cried the cat, 'one word more and I will eat you too.'

'All gone' was already on the poor mouse's lips; scarcely had she spoken it before the cat sprang on her, seized her, and swallowed her down. Verily, that is the way of the world.

THE STORY OF THE YOUTH WHO WENT FORTH TO LEARN WHAT FEAR WAS

A certain father had two sons, the elder of whom was sharp and sensible, and could do everything, but the younger was stupid and could neither learn nor understand anything, and when people saw him they said, 'There's a fellow who will give his father some trouble!' When anything had to be done, it was always the elder who was forced to do it; but if his father bade him fetch anything when it was late, or in the night-time, and the way led through the churchyard, or any other dismal place, he answered 'Oh, no, father, I'll not go there, it makes me shudder!' for he was afraid. Or when stories were told by the fire at night which made the flesh creep, the listeners often said, 'Oh, it makes us shudder!' The younger sat in a corner and listened with the rest of them, and could not imagine what they could mean. 'They are always saying, "It makes me shudder, it makes me shudder!" It does not make me shudder,' thought he. 'That, too, must be an art of which I understand nothing.'

Now it came to pass that his father said to him one day, 'Hearken to me, thou fellow in the corner there, thou art growing tall and strong, and thou too must learn something by which thou canst earn thy living. Look how thy brother works, but thou dost not even earn thy salt.'

'Well, father,' he replied, 'I am quite willing to learn something – indeed, if it could but be managed, I should like to learn how to shudder. I don't understand that at all yet.'

The elder brother smiled when he heard that, and thought to himself, 'Good God, what a blockhead that brother of mine is! He will never be good for anything as long as he lives. He who wants to be a sickle must bend himself betimes.'

The father sighed, and answered him: 'Thou shalt soon learn what it is to shudder, but thou wilt not earn thy living by that.'

Soon after this the sexton came to the house on a visit, and the father bewailed his trouble, and told him how his younger son was so backward in every respect that he knew nothing and learnt nothing. 'Just think,' said he, 'when I asked him how he was going to earn his bread, he actually wanted to learn to shudder."

'If that be all,' replied the sexton, 'he can learn that with me. Send him to me, and I will soon polish him.'

The father was glad to do it, for he thought, 'It will train the boy a little.' The sexton therefore took him into his house, and he had to ring the bell. After a day or two, the sexton awoke him at midnight, and bade him arise and go up into the church tower and ring the bell. 'Thou shalt soon learn what shuddering is,' thought he, and secretly went there before him; and when the boy was at the top of the tower and turned round, and was just going to take hold of the bell rope, he saw a white figure standing on the stairs opposite the sounding hole. 'Who is there?' cried he, but the figure made no reply, and did not move or stir. 'Give an answer,' cried the boy, 'or take thy self off, thou hast no business here at night.'

The sexton, however, remained standing motionless that the boy might think he was a ghost. The boy cried a second time, 'What do you want here? – speak if thou art an honest fellow, or I will throw thee down the steps!'

The sexton thought, 'he can't intend to be as bad as his words,' uttered no sound and stood as if he were made of stone. Then the boy called to him for the third time, and as that was also to no purpose, he ran against him and pushed the ghost down the stairs, so that it fell down ten steps and remained lying there in a corner. Thereupon he rang the bell, went home, and without saying a word went to bed, and fell asleep. The sexton's wife waited a long time for her husband, but he did not come back. At length she became uneasy, and wakened the boy, and asked, 'Dost thou not know where my husband is? He climbed up the tower before thou didst.'

'No, I don't know,' replied the boy, 'but someone was standing by the sounding hole on the other side of the steps, and as he would neither give an answer nor go away, I took him for a scoundrel, and threw him downstairs, just go there and you will see if it was he. I should be sorry if it were.'

The woman ran away and found her husband, who was lying moaning in the corner, and had broken his leg.

She carried him down, and then with loud screams she hastened to the boy's father. 'Your boy,' cried she, 'has been the cause of a great misfortune! He has thrown my husband down the steps and made him break his leg. Take the good-for-nothing fellow away from our house.'

The father was terrified, and ran thither and scolded the boy. 'What wicked tricks are these?' said he, 'the devil must have put this into thy head.'

'Father,' he replied, 'do listen to me. I am quite innocent. He was standing there by night like one who is intending to do some evil. I did not know who it was, and I entreated him three times either to speak or to go away.'

'Ah,' said the father, 'I have nothing but unhappiness with you. Go out of my sight. I will see thee no more.'

'Yes, father, right willingly, wait only until it is day. Then will I go forth and learn how to shudder, and then I shall, at any rate, understand one art which will support me.'

'Learn what thou wilt,' spake the father, 'it is all the same to me. Here are fifty thalers for thee. Take these and go into the wide world, and tell no one from whence thou comest, and who is thy father, for I have reason to be ashamed of thee.'

'Yes, father, it shall be as you will. If you desire nothing more than that, I can easily keep it in mind.'

When day dawned, therefore, the boy put his fifty thalers into his pocket, and went forth on the great highway, and continually said to himself, 'If I could but shudder! If I could but shudder!' Then a man approached who heard this conversation which the youth was holding with himself, and when they had walked a little farther to where they could see the gallows, the man said to him, 'Look, there is the tree where seven men have married the ropemaker's daughter, and are now learning how to fly. Sit down below it, and wait till night comes, and you will soon learn how to shudder.'

'If that is all that is wanted,' answered the youth, 'it is easily done; but if I learn how to shudder as fast as that, thou shalt have my fifty thalers. Just come back to me early in the morning.' Then the youth went to the gallows, sat down below it, and waited till evening came. And as he was cold, he lighted himself a fire, but at midnight the wind blew so sharply that in spite of his fire, he could not get warm. And as the wind knocked the hanged men against each other, and they moved backwards and forwards, he thought to himself, 'Thou shiverest below by the fire, but how those up above must freeze and suffer!' And as he felt pity for them, he raised the ladder, and climbed up, unbound one of them after the other, and brought down all seven. Then he stirred the fire, blew it, and set them all round it to warm themselves. But they sat there and did not stir, and the fire caught their clothes. So he said, 'Take care, or I will hang you up again.' The dead men, however, did not hear, but were quite silent, and let their rags go on burning. On this he grew angry, and said, 'If you will not take care, I cannot help you, I will not be burnt with you,' and he hung them up again each in his turn. Then he sat down by his fire and fell asleep, and the next morning the man came to him and wanted to have the fifty thalers, and said, 'Well, dost thou know how to shudder?'

'No,' answered he, 'how was I to get to know? Those fellows up there did not open their mouths, and were so stupid that they let the few old rags which they had on their bodies get burnt.' Then the man saw that he would not get the fifty thalers that day, and went away saying, 'One of this kind has never come my way before.'

The youth likewise went his way, and once more began to mutter to himself, 'Ah, if I could but shudder! Ah, if I could but shudder!'

A waggoner who was striding behind him heard that and asked, 'Who are you?'

'I don't know,' answered the youth.

Then the waggoner asked, 'From whence comest thou?'

'I know not.'

'Who is thy father?'

'That I may not tell thee.'

'What is it that thou art always muttering between thy teeth?'

'Ah,' replied the youth, 'I do so wish I could shudder, but no one can teach me how to do it.'

'Give up thy foolish chatter,' said the waggoner. 'Come, go with me, I will see about a place for thee.'

The youth went with the waggoner, and in the evening they arrived at an inn where they wished to pass the night. Then at the entrance of the room the youth again said quite loudly, 'If I could but shudder! If I could but shudder!' The host who heard this, laughed and said, 'If that is your desire, there ought to be a good opportunity for you here.'

'Ah, be silent,' said the hostess, 'so many inquisitive persons have already lost their lives, it would be a pity and a shame if such beautiful eyes as these should never see the daylight again.'

But the youth said, 'However difficult it may be, I will learn it and for this purpose indeed have I journeyed forth.' He let the host have no rest, until the latter told him, that not far from thence stood a haunted castle where anyone could very easily learn what shuddering was, if he would but watch in it for three nights. The King had promised that he who would venture should have his daughter to wife, and she was the most beautiful maiden the sun shone on. Great treasures likewise lay in the castle, which were guarded by evil spirits, and these treasures would then be freed, and would make a poor man rich enough. Already many men had gone into the castle, but as yet none had come out again.

Then the youth went next morning to the King and said if he were allowed he would watch three nights in the haunted castle. The King looked at him, and as the youth pleased him, he said, 'Thou mayest ask for three things to take into the castle with thee, but they must be things without life.' Then he answered, 'Then I ask for a fire, a turning lathe, and a cutting-board with the knife.'

The King had these things carried into the castle for him during the day. When night was drawing near, the youth went up and made himself a bright fire in one of the rooms, placed the cutting-board and knife beside it, and seated himself by the turning-lathe. 'Ah, if I could but shudder!' said he, 'but I shall not learn it here either.'

Towards midnight he was about to poke his fire, and as he was blowing it, something cried suddenly from one corner, 'Au, miau! how cold we are!'

'You simpletons!' cried he, 'what are you crying about? If you are cold, come and take a seat by the fire and warm yourselves.' And when he had said that, two great black cats came with one tremendous leap and sat down on each side of him, and looked savagely at him with their fiery eyes. After a short time, when they had warmed themselves, they said, 'Comrade, shall we have a game at cards?'

'Why not?' he replied, 'but just show me your paws.'

Then they stretched out their claws. 'Oh,' said he, 'what long nails you have! Wait, I must first cut them for you.' Thereupon he seized them by the throats, put them on the cutting-board and screwed their feet fast. 'I have looked at your fingers,' said he, 'and my fancy for card-playing has gone,' and he struck them dead and threw them out into the water. But when he had made away with these two, and was about to sit down again by his fire, out from every hole and corner came black cats and black dogs with red-hot chains, and more and more of them came until he could no longer stir, and they yelled horribly, and got on his fire, pulled it to pieces, and tried to put it out. He watched them for a while quietly, but at last when they were going too far, he seized his cutting-knife, and cried, 'Away with ye, vermin,' and began to cut them down.

Part of them ran away, the others he killed, and threw out into the fishpond. When he came back he blew up the embers of his fire again and warmed himself. And as he thus sat, his eyes would keep open no longer, and he felt a desire to sleep. Then he looked round and saw a great bed in the corner. 'That is the very thing for me,' said he, and got into it. When he was just going to shut his eyes, however, the bed began to move of its own accord, and went over the whole of the castle. 'That's right,' said he, 'but go faster.' Then the bed rolled on as if six horses were harnessed to it, up and down, over thresholds and steps, but suddenly hop, hop, it turned over upside down, and lay on him like a mountain. But he threw quilts and pillows up in the air, got out and said, 'Now any one who likes, may drive,' and lay down by his fire, and slept till it was day.

In the morning the King came, and when he saw him lying there on the ground, he thought the evil spirits had killed him and he was dead. Then said he, 'After all it is a pity – he is a handsome man.' The youth heard it, got up, and said, 'It has not come to that yet.' Then the King was astonished, but very glad, and asked how he had fared. 'Very well indeed,' answered he; 'one night is past, the two others will get over likewise.' Then he went to the innkeeper, who opened his eyes very wide, and said, 'I never expected to see thee alive again! Hast thou learnt how to shudder yet?'

'No,' said he, 'it is all in vain. If someone would but tell me.'

The second night he again went up into the old castle, sat down by the fire, and once more began his old song, 'If I could but shudder.' When midnight came, an uproar and noise of tumbling about was heard; at first it was low, but it grew louder and louder.

Then it was quiet for a while, and at length with a loud scream, half a man came down the chimney and fell before him. 'Hello!' cried he, 'another half belongs to this. This is too little!' Then the uproar began again, there was a roaring and howling, and the other half fell down likewise. 'Wait,' said he, 'I will just blow up the fire a little for thee.'

When he had done that and looked round again, the two pieces were joined together, and a frightful man was sitting in his place. 'That is no part of our bargain,' said the youth, 'the bench is mine.' The man wanted to push him away; the youth, however, would not allow that, but thrust him off with all his strength, and seated himself again in his own place. Then still more men fell down, one after the other; they brought nine dead men's legs and two skulls, and set them up and played at nine-pins with them. The youth also wanted to play and said, 'Hark you, can I join you?'

'Yes, if thou hast any money.'

'Money enough,' replied he, 'but your balls are not quite round.'

Then he took the skulls and put them in the lathe and turned them till they were round. 'There, now, they will roll better!' said he. 'Hurrah! Now it goes merrily!' He played with them and lost some of his money, but when it struck twelve, everything vanished from his sight. He lay down and quietly fell asleep.

Next morning the King came to enquire after him. 'How has it fared with you this time?' asked he.

'I have been playing at nine-pins,' he answered, 'and have lost a couple of farthings.'

'Hast thou not shuddered then?'

'Eh, what?' said he, 'I have made merry. If I did but know what it was to shudder!'

THE STORY OF THE YOUTH

The third night he sat down again on his bench and said quite sadly, 'If I could but shudder.'

When it grew late, six tall men came in and brought a coffin. Then said he, 'Ha, ha, that is certainly my little cousin, who died only a few days ago,' and he beckoned with his finger, and cried, 'Come, little cousin, come.'

They placed the coffin on the ground, but he went to it and took the lid off, and a dead man lay therein. He felt his face, but it was cold as ice. 'Stop,' said he, 'I will warm thee a little,' and went to the fire and warmed his hand and laid it on the dead man's face, but he remained cold. Then he took him out, and sat down by the fire and laid him on his breast and rubbed his arms that the blood might circulate again. As this also did no good, he thought to himself, 'When two people lie in bed together, they warm each other,' and carried him to the bed, covered him over and lay down by him. After a short time the dead man became warm, too, and began to move. Then said the youth, 'See, little cousin, have I not warmed thee?'

The dead man, however, got up and cried, 'Now will I strangle thee.'

'What!' said he, 'is that the way thou thankest me? Thou shalt at once go into thy coffin again,' and he took him up, threw him into it, and shut the lid. Then came the six men and carried him away again. 'I cannot manage to shudder,' said he. 'I shall never learn it here as long as I live.'

Then a man entered who was taller than all others, and looked terrible. He was old, however, and had a long white beard. 'Thou wretch,' cried he, 'thou shalt soon learn what it is to shudder, for thou shalt die.'

'Not so fast,' replied the youth. 'If I am to die, I shall have to have a say in it.'

'I will soon seize thee,' said the fiend.

'Softly, softly, do not talk so big. I am as strong as thou art, and perhaps even stronger.'

'We shall see,' said the old man. 'If thou art stronger, I will let thee go – come, we will try.' Then he led him by dark passages to a smith's forge, took an axe, and with one blow struck an anvil into the ground.

'I can do better than that,' said the youth, and went to the other anvil.

The old man placed himself near and wanted to look on, and his white beard hung down. Then the youth seized the axe, split the anvil with one blow, and struck the old man's beard in with it. 'Now I have thee,' said the youth. 'Now it is thou who will have to die.' Then he seized an iron bar and beat the old man till he moaned and entreated him to stop, and he would give him great riches. The youth drew out the axe and let him go.

The old man led him back into the castle, and in a cellar showed him three chests full of gold. 'Of these,' said he, 'one part is for the poor, the other for the king, the third is thine.'

In the meantime, it struck twelve, and the spirit disappeared; the youth, therefore, was left in darkness. 'I shall still be able to find my way out,' said he, and felt about, found the way into the room, and slept there by his fire.

Next morning, the King came and said, 'Now thou must have learnt what shuddering is?'

'No,' he answered; 'what can it be? My dead cousin was here, and a bearded man came and showed me a great deal of money down below, but no one told me what it was to shudder.'

'Then,' said the King, 'thou hast delivered the castle, and shalt marry my daughter.'

'That is all very well,' said he, 'but still I do not know what it is to shudder.'

Then the gold was brought up and the wedding celebrated; but howsoever much the young king loved his wife, and however happy he was, he still said always, 'If I could but shudder – if I could but shudder.' And at length she was angry at this. Her waiting-maid said, 'I will find a cure for him; he shall soon learn what it is to shudder.' She went out to the stream which flowed through the garden, and had a whole bucketful of gudgeons brought to her. At night when the young king was sleeping, his wife was to draw the clothes off him and empty the bucketful of cold water with the gudgeons in it over him, so that the little fishes would sprawl about him. When this was done, he woke up and cried, 'Oh, what makes me shudder so? – what makes me shudder so, dear wife? Ah! Now I know what it is to shudder!'

THE WONDERFUL MUSICIAN

There was once a wonderful musician, who went quite alone through a forest and thought of all manner of things, and when nothing was left for him to think about, he said to himself, 'Time is beginning to pass heavily with me here in the forest, I will fetch hither a good companion for myself.' Then he took his fiddle from his back, and played so that it echoed through the trees.

It was not long before a wolf came trotting through the thicket towards him. 'Ah, here is a wolf coming! I have no desire for him!' said the musician; but the wolf came nearer and said to him, 'Ah, dear musician, how beautifully thou dost play. I should like to learn that, too.'

'It is soon learnt,' the musician replied, 'thou hast only to do all that I bid thee.'

'Oh, musician,' said the wolf, 'I will obey thee as a scholar obeys his master.'

The musician bade him follow, and when they had gone part of the way together, they came to an old oak tree which was hollow inside, and cleft in the middle. 'Look,' said the musician, 'if thou wilt learn to fiddle, put thy fore paws into this crevice.' The wolf obeyed, but the musician quickly picked up a stone and with one blow wedged his two paws so fast that he was forced to stay there like a prisoner. 'Stay there until I come back again,' said the musician, and went his way.

After a while he again said to himself, 'Time is beginning to pass heavily with me here in the forest, I will fetch hither another companion,' and took his fiddle and again played in the forest. It was not long before a fox came creeping through the trees towards him. 'Ah, there's a fox coming!' said the musician. 'I have no desire for him.'

The fox came up to him and said, 'Oh, dear musician, how beautifully thou dost play! I should like to learn that too.'

'That is soon learnt,' said the musician. 'Thou hast only to do everything that I bid thee.'

'Oh, musician,' then said the fox, 'I will obey thee as a scholar obeys his master.'

'Follow me,' said the musician; and when they had walked a part of the way, they came to a footpath, with high bushes on both sides of it. There the musician stood still, and from one side bent a young hazel bush down to the ground, and put his foot on the top of it, then he bent down a young tree from the other side as well, and said, 'Now little fox, if thou wilt learn something, give me thy left front paw.' The fox obeyed, and the musician fastened his paw to the left bough. 'Little fox,' said he, 'now reach me thy right paw,' and he tied it to the right bough. When he had examined whether they were firm enough, he let go, and the bushes sprang up again, and jerked up the little fox, so that it hung struggling in the air. 'Wait there till I come back again,' said the musician, and went his way.

Again he said to himself, 'Time is beginning to pass heavily with me here in the forest, I will fetch hither another companion,' so he took his fiddle, and the sound echoed through the forest. Then a little hare came springing towards him. 'Why, a hare is coming,' said the musician, 'I do not want him.'

'Ah, dear musician,' said the hare, 'how beautifully thou dost fiddle; I too, should like to learn that.'

'That is soon learnt,' said the musician, 'thou hast only to do everything that I bid thee.'

'Oh, musician,' replied the little hare, 'I will obey thee as a scholar obeys his master.'

They went a part of the way together until they came to an open space in the forest, where stood an aspen tree. The musician tied a long string round the little hare's neck, the other end of which he fastened to the tree. 'Now briskly, little hare, run twenty times round the tree!' cried the musician, and the little hare obeyed, and when it had run round twenty times, it had twisted the string twenty times round the trunk of the tree, and the little hare was caught, and let it pull and tug as it liked, it only made the string cut into its tender neck. 'Wait there till I come back,' said the musician, and went onwards.

The wolf, in the meantime, had pushed and pulled and bitten at the stone, and had worked so long that he had set his feet at liberty and had drawn them once more out of the cleft. Full of anger and rage he hurried after the musician and wanted to tear him to pieces. When the fox saw him running, he began to lament, and cried with all his might, 'Brother wolf, come to my help, the musician has betrayed me!' The wolf drew down the little tree, bit the cord in two, and freed the fox, who went with him to take revenge on the musician. They found the tied-up hare, whom likewise they delivered, and then they all sought the enemy together.

The musician had once more played his fiddle as he went on his way, and this time he had been more fortunate. The sound reached the ears of a poor wood-cutter, who instantly, whether he would or no, gave up his work and came with his hatchet under his arm to listen to the music. 'At last comes the right companion,' said the musician, 'for I was seeking a human being, and no wild beast.' And he began and played so beautifully and delightfully that the poor man stood there as if bewitched, and his heart leaped with gladness. And as he thus stood, the wolf, the fox, and the hare came up, and he saw well that they had some evil design. So he raised his glittering axe and placed himself before the musician, as if to say, 'Whoso wishes to touch him let him beware, for he will have to do with me!' Then the beasts were terrified and ran back into the forest. The musician, however, played once more to the man out of gratitude, and then went onwards.

THE TWELVE BROTHERS

There were once upon a time a king and a queen who lived happily together and had twelve children, but they were all boys. Then said the King to his wife, 'If the thirteenth child which thou art about to bring into the world, is a girl, the twelve boys shall die, in order that her possessions may be great, and that the kingdom may fall to her alone.' He caused likewise twelve coffins to be made, which were already filled with shavings, and in each lay the little pillow for the dead, and he had them taken into a locked-up room, and then he gave the Queen the key of it, and bade her not to speak of this to any one.

The mother, however, now sat and lamented all day long, until the youngest son, who was always with her, and whom she had named Benjamin, from the Bible, said to her, 'Dear mother, why art thou so sad?'

'Dearest child,' she answered, 'I may not tell thee.'

But he let her have no rest until she went and unlocked the room, and showed him the twelve coffins ready filled with shavings. Then she said, 'My dearest Benjamin, thy father has had these coffins made for thee and for thy eleven brothers, for if I bring a little girl into the world, you are all to be killed and buried in them.' And as she wept while she was saying this, the son comforted her and said, 'Weep not, dear mother, we will save ourselves, and go hence.'

But she said, 'Go forth into the forest with thy eleven brothers, and let one sit constantly on the highest tree which can be found, and keep watch, looking towards the tower here in the castle. If I give birth to a little son, I will put up a white flag, and then you may venture to come back, but if I bear a daughter, I will hoist a red flag, and then fly hence as quickly as you are able, and may the good God protect you. And every night I will rise up and pray for you – in winter that you may be able to warm yourself at a fire, and in summer that you may not faint away in the heat.'

After she had blessed her sons therefore, they went forth into the forest. They each kept watch in turn, and sat on the highest oak and looked towards the tower. When eleven days had passed and the turn came to Benjamin, he saw that a flag was being raised. It was, however, not the white, but the blood-red flag that announced that they were all to die. When the brothers heard that, they were very angry and said, 'Are we all to suffer death for the sake of a girl? We swear that we will avenge ourselves! – wheresoever we find a girl, her red blood shall flow.'

Thereupon they went deeper into the forest, and in the midst of it, where it was the darkest, they found a little bewitched hut, which was standing empty. Then said they, 'Here we will dwell, and thou Benjamin, who art the youngest and weakest, thou shalt stay at home and keep house, we others will go out and get food.' Then they went into the forest and shot hares, wild deer, birds and pigeons, and whatsoever there was to eat; this they took to Benjamin, who had to dress it for them in order that they might appease their hunger. They lived together ten years in the little hut, and the time did not appear long to them.

The little daughter, which their mother the Queen had given birth to, was now grown up; she was good of heart, and fair of face, and had a golden star on her forehead. Once, when it was the great washing, she saw twelve men's shirts among the things, and asked her mother, 'To whom do these twelve shirts belong, for they are far too small for father?' Then the Queen answered with a heavy heart, 'Dear child, these belong to thy twelve brothers.' Said the maiden, 'Where are my twelve brothers, I have never yet heard of them?'

She replied, 'God knows where they are, they are wandering about the world.' Then she took the maiden and opened the chamber for her, and showed her the twelve coffins with the shavings, and pillows for the head. 'These coffins,' said she, 'were destined for thy brothers, but they went away secretly before thou wert born,' and she related to her how everything had happened; then said the maiden, 'Dear mother, weep not, I will go and seek my brothers.'

So she took the twelve shirts and went forth, and straight into the great forest. She walked the whole day, and in the evening she came to the bewitched hut. Then she entered it and found a young boy, who asked, 'From whence comest thou, and whither art thou bound?' and was astonished that she was so beautiful, and wore royal garments, and had a star on her forehead. And she answered, 'I am a king's daughter, and am seeking my twelve brothers, and I will walk as far as the sky is blue until I find them.' She likewise showed him the twelve shirts which belonged to them. Then Benjamin saw that she was his sister, and said, 'I am Benjamin, thy youngest brother.' And she began to weep for joy, and Benjamin wept also, and they kissed and embraced each other with the greatest love. But after this he said, 'Dear sister, there is still one difficulty. We have agreed that every maiden whom we meet shall die, because we have been obliged to leave our kingdom on account of a girl.' Then said she, 'I will willingly die, if by so doing I can deliver my twelve brothers.'

'No,' answered he, 'thou shalt not die, seat thyself beneath this tub until our eleven brothers come, and then I will soon come to an agreement with them.'

She did so, and when it was night the others came from hunting, and their dinner was ready. And as they were sitting at table, and eating, they asked, 'What news is there?'

Said Benjamin, 'Don't you know anything?'

'No,' they answered.

He continued, 'You have been in the forest and I have stayed at home, and yet I know more than you do.'

'Tell us then,' they cried.

He answered, 'But promise me that the first maiden who meets us shall not be killed.'

'Yes,' they all cried, 'she shall have mercy, only do tell us.'

Then said he, 'Our sister is here,' and he lifted up the tub, and the King's daughter came forth in her royal garments with the golden star on her forehead, and she was beautiful, delicate and fair. Then they were all rejoiced, and fell on her neck, and kissed and loved her with all their hearts.

Now she stayed at home with Benjamin and helped him with the work. The eleven went into the forest and caught game, and deer, and birds, and woodpigeons that they might have food, and the little sister and Benjamin took care to make it ready for them. She sought for the wood for cooking and herbs for vegetables, and put the pans on the fire so that the dinner was always ready when the eleven came. She likewise kept order in the little house, and put beautifully white clean coverings on the little beds, and the brothers were always contented and lived in great harmony with her.

Once upon a time the two at home had prepared a beautiful

entertainment, and when they were all together, they sat down and ate and drank and were full of gladness. There was, however, a little garden belonging to the bewitched house wherein stood twelve lily flowers, which are likewise called students.[1] She wished to give her brothers pleasure, and plucked the twelve flowers, and thought she would present each brother with one while at dinner. But at the self-same moment that she plucked the flowers, the twelve brothers were changed into twelve ravens, and flew away over the forest, and the house and garden vanished likewise. And now the poor maiden was alone in the wild forest, and when she looked around, an old woman was standing near her who said, 'My child, what hast thou done? Why didst thou not leave the twelve white flowers growing? They were thy brothers, who are now for evermore changed into ravens.' The maiden said, weeping, 'Is there no way of delivering them?'

'No,' said the woman, 'there is but one in the whole world, and that is so hard that thou wilt not deliver them by it, for thou must be dumb for seven years, and mayst not speak or laugh, and if thou speakest one single word, and only an hour of the seven years is wanting, all is in vain, and thy brothers will be killed by the one word.'

Then said the maiden in her heart, 'I know with certainty that I shall set my brothers free,' and went and sought a high tree and seated herself in it and span, and neither spoke nor laughed. Now it so happened that a king was hunting in the forest, who had a great greyhound which ran to the tree on which the maiden was sitting, and sprang about it, whining, and barking at her. Then the King came by and saw the beautiful King's daughter with the golden star on her brow, and was so charmed with her beauty that he called to ask her if she would be his wife. She made no answer,

---

[1] *Studenten-Nelken*, or *Studenten-Lilien*, are a species of small pinks, and are so called because they are much worn by the students of various universities, in the buttonhole of their coats. They are sometimes called *Federnelken* (Feather-pink, or 'sop in the wine'). The brothers Grimm themselves, in the notes to 'De drei Vügelkens', speak of this flower as the narcissus.

but nodded a little with her head. So he climbed up the tree himself, carried her down, placed her on his horse, and bore her home.

Then the wedding was solemnized with great magnificence and rejoicing, but the bride neither spoke nor smiled. When they had lived happily together for a few years, the King's mother, who was a wicked woman, began to slander the young Queen, and said to the King, 'This is a common beggar girl whom thou hast brought back with thee. Who knows what impious tricks she practises secretly! Even if she be dumb, and not able to speak, she still might laugh for once; but those who do not laugh have bad consciences.'

At first the King would not believe it, but the old woman urged this so long, and accused her of so many evil things, that at last the King let himself be persuaded and sentenced her to death.

And now a great fire was lit in the courtyard in which she was to be burnt, and the King stood above at the window and looked on with tearful eyes, because he still loved her so much. And when she was bound fast to the stake, and the fire was licking at her clothes with its red tongue, the last instant of the seven years expired. Then a whirring sound was heard in the air, and twelve ravens came flying towards the place, and sank downwards, and when they touched the earth they were her twelve brothers, whom she had delivered. They tore the fire asunder, extinguished the flames, set their dear sister free, and kissed and embraced her. And now as she dared to open her mouth and speak, she told the King why she had been dumb, and had never laughed. The King rejoiced when he heard that she was innocent, and they all lived in great unity until their death. The wicked step-mother was taken before the judge, and put into a barrel filled with boiling oil and venomous snakes, and died an evil death.

RAPUNZEL[1]

There were once a man and a woman who had long in vain wished for a child. At length the woman hoped that God was about to grant her desire. These people had a little window at the back of their house from which a splendid garden could be seen, which was full of the most beautiful flowers and herbs. It was, however, surrounded by a high wall, and no one dared to go into it because it belonged to an enchantress, who had great power and was dreaded by all the world. One day the woman was standing by this window and looking down into the garden, when she saw a bed which was planted with the most beautiful rampion (rapunzel), and it looked so fresh and green that she longed for it, and had the greatest desire to eat some. This desire increased every day, and as she knew that she could not get any of it, she quite pined away, and looked pale and miserable. Then her husband was alarmed, and asked, 'What aileth thee, dear wife?'

'Ah,' she replied, 'if I can't get some of the rampion, which is in the garden behind our house, to eat, I shall die.'

The man, who loved her, thought, 'Sooner than let thy wife die, bring her some of the rampion thyself, let it cost thee what it will.' In the twilight of the evening, he clambered down over the wall into the garden of the enchantress, hastily clutched a handful of rampion, and took it to his wife. She at once made herself a salad of it, and ate it with much relish. She, however, liked it so much – so very much – that the next day she longed

---

[1] Rapunzel, Campanula *rapunculus* (rampion), is a congener of the common harebell. It has a long white spindle-shaped root, which is eaten raw like a radish and has a pleasant sweet flavour. Its leaves and young shoots are also used in salads and so are the roots, sliced.

for it three times as much as before. If he was to have any rest, her husband must once more descend into the garden. In the gloom of evening, therefore, he let himself down again; but when he had clambered down the wall he was terribly afraid, for he saw the enchantress standing before him.

'How canst thou dare,' said she with angry look, 'to descend into my garden and steal my rampion like a thief? Thou shalt suffer for it!'

'Ah,' answered he, 'let mercy take the place of justice, I only made up my mind to do it out of necessity. My wife saw your rampion from the window, and felt such a longing for it that she would have died if she had not got some to eat.'

Then the enchantress allowed her anger to be softened, and said to him, 'If the case be as thou sayest, I will allow thee to take away with thee as much rampion as thou wilt, only I make one condition, thou must give me the child which thy wife will bring into the world; it shall be well treated, and I will care for it like a mother.'

The man in his terror consented to everything, and when the woman was brought to bed, the enchantress appeared at once, gave the child the name of Rapunzel, and took it away with her.

Rapunzel grew into the most beautiful child beneath the sun. When she was twelve years old, the enchantress shut her into a tower, which lay in a forest, and had neither stairs nor door, but quite at the top was a little window. When the enchantress wanted to go in, she placed herself beneath it and cried,

'Rapunzel, Rapunzel,

Let down thy hair to me.'

Rapunzel had magnificent long hair, fine as spun gold, and when she heard the voice of the enchantress she unfastened her braided tresses, wound them round one of the hooks of the window above, and then the hair fell twenty ells down, and the enchantress climbed up by it.

After a year or two, it came to pass that the King's son rode through the forest and went by the tower. Then he heard a song, which was so charming that he stood still and listened. This was Rapunzel, who in her solitude passed her time in letting her sweet voice resound. The King's son wanted to climb up to her, and looked for the door of the tower, but none was to be found. He rode home, but the singing had so deeply touched his heart, that every day he went out into the forest and listened to it. Once when he was thus standing behind a tree, he saw that an enchantress came there, and he heard how she cried,

'Rapunzel, Rapunzel,
Let down thy hair.'

Then Rapunzel let down the braids of her hair, and the enchantress climbed up to her. 'If that is the ladder by which one mounts, I will for once try my fortune,' said he, and the next day when it began to grow dark, he went to the tower and cried,

'Rapunzel, Rapunzel,
Let down thy hair.'

Immediately the hair fell down and the King's son climbed up.

At first Rapunzel was terribly frightened when a man such as her eyes had never yet beheld, came to her; but the King's son began to talk to her quite like a friend, and told her that his heart had been so stirred that it had let him have no rest, and he had been forced to see her. Then Rapunzel lost her fear, and when he asked her if she would take him for her husband, and she saw that he was young and handsome, she thought, 'He will love me more than old Dame Gothel does,' and she said yes, and laid her hand in his.

She said, 'I will willingly go away with thee, but I do not know how to get down. Bring with thee a skein of silk every time that thou comest, and I will weave a ladder with it, and when that is ready I will descend, and thou wilt take me on thy horse.' They agreed that until that time he should come to her every evening, for the old woman came by day. The enchantress remarked nothing of this, until once Rapunzel said to her, 'Tell me, Dame Gothel, how it happens that you are so much heavier for me to draw up than the young King's son – he is with me in a moment.'

'Ah! thou wicked child,' cried the enchantress. 'What do I hear thee say! I thought I had separated thee from all the world, and yet thou hast deceived me.' In her anger she clutched Rapunzel's beautiful tresses, wrapped them twice round her left hand, seized a pair of scissors with the right, and snip, snap, they were cut off, and the lovely braids lay on the ground. And she was so pitiless that she took poor Rapunzel into a desert where she had to live in great grief and misery.

On the same day, however, that she cast out Rapunzel, the enchantress in the evening fastened the braids of hair which she had cut off, to the hook of the window, and when the King's son came and cried,

'Rapunzel, Rapunzel,
Let down thy hair,'

she let the hair down. The King's son ascended, but he did not find his dearest Rapunzel above, but the enchantress, who gazed at him with wicked and venomous looks. 'Aha!' she cried mockingly, 'Thou wouldst fetch thy dearest, but the beautiful bird sits no longer singing in the nest; the cat has got it, and will scratch out thy eyes as well. Rapunzel is lost to thee; thou wilt never see her more.'

The King's son was beside himself with pain, and in his despair he leapt down from the tower. He escaped with his life, but the thorns into which he fell, pierced his eyes. Then he wandered quite blind about the forest, ate nothing but roots and berries, and did nothing but lament and weep over the loss of his dearest wife. Thus he roamed about in misery for some years, and at length came to the desert where Rapunzel, with the twins to which she had given birth, a boy and a girl, lived in wretchedness. He heard a voice, and it seemed so familiar to him that he went towards it, and when he approached, Rapunzel knew him and fell on his neck and wept. Two of her tears wetted his eyes and they grew clear again, and he could see with them as before. He led her to his kingdom where he was joyfully received, and they lived for a long time afterwards, happy and contented.

THE THREE SPINNERS

There was once a girl who was idle and would not spin, and let her mother say what she would, she could not bring her to it. At last, the mother was once so overcome with anger and impatience, that she beat her, on which the girl began to weep loudly. Now, at this very moment, the Queen drove by, and when she heard the weeping she stopped her carriage, went into the house and asked the mother why she was beating her daughter so that the cries could be heard out on the road? Then the woman was ashamed to reveal the laziness of her daughter and said, 'I cannot get her to leave off spinning. She insists on spinning for ever and ever, and I am poor, and cannot procure the flax.'

Then answered the Queen, 'There is nothing that I like better to hear than spinning, and I am never happier than when the wheels are humming. Let me have your daughter with me in the palace. I have flax enough, and there she shall spin as much as she likes.'

The mother was heartily satisfied with this, and the Queen took the girl with her. When they had arrived at the palace, she led her up into three rooms which were filled from the bottom to the top with the finest flax. 'Now spin me this flax,' said she, 'and when thou hast done it, thou shalt have my eldest son for a husband, even if thou art poor. I care not for that, thy indefatigable industry is dowry enough.'

The girl was secretly terrified, for she could not have spun the flax, no, not if she had lived till she was three hundred years old, and had sat at it every day from morning till night. When therefore she was alone, she began to weep, and sat thus for three days without moving a finger. On the third day came the Queen, and when she saw that nothing had been spun yet, she was surprised; but the girl excused herself by saying that she had not been able to begin because of her great distress at leaving her mother's house. The queen was satisfied with this, but said when she was going away, 'Tomorrow thou must begin to work.'

When the girl was alone again, she did not know what to do, and in her distress went to the window. Then she saw three women coming towards her, the first of whom had a broad flat foot, the second had such a great underlip that it hung down over her chin, and the third had a broad thumb. They remained standing before the window, looked up, and asked the girl what was amiss with her?

She complained of her trouble, and then they offered her their help and said, 'If thou wilt invite us to the wedding, not be ashamed of us, and wilt call us thine aunts, and likewise wilt place us at thy table, we will spin up the flax for thee, and that in a very short time.'

'With all my heart,' she replied, 'do but come in and begin the work at once.'

Then she let in the three strange women, and cleared a place in the first room, where they seated themselves and began their spinning. The one drew the thread and trod the wheel, the other wetted the thread, the third twisted it, and struck the table with her finger, and as often as she struck it, a skein of thread fell to the ground that was spun in the finest manner possible. The girl concealed the three spinners from the Queen, and showed her whenever she came the great quantity of spun thread, until the latter could not praise her enough. When the first room was empty she went to the second, and at last to the third, and that too was quickly cleared. Then the three women took leave and said to the girl, 'Do not forget what thou hast promised us – it will make thy fortune.'

When the maiden showed the Queen the empty rooms, and the great heap of yarn, she gave orders for the wedding, and the bridegroom rejoiced that he was to have such a clever and industrious wife, and praised her mightily. 'I have three aunts,' said the girl, 'and as they have been very kind to me, I should not like to forget them in my good fortune; allow me to invite them to the wedding, and let them sit with us at table.'

The Queen and the bridegroom said, 'Why should we not allow that?'

Therefore, when the feast began, the three women entered in strange apparel, and the bride said, 'Welcome, dear aunts.'

'Ah,' said the bridegroom, 'how comest thou by these odious friends?' Thereupon he went to the one with the broad flat foot, and said, 'How do you come by such a broad foot?'

'By treading,' she answered, 'by treading.'

Then the bridegroom went to the second, and said, 'How do you come by your falling lip?'

'By licking,' she answered, 'by licking.'

Then he asked the third, 'How do you come by your broad thumb?'

'By twisting the thread,' she answered, 'by twisting the thread.'

On this the King's son was alarmed and said, 'Neither now nor ever shall my beautiful bride touch a spinning-wheel.' And thus she got rid of the hateful flax-spinning.

HANSEL AND GRETHEL

Hard by a great forest dwelt a poor wood-cutter with his wife and his two children. The boy was called Hansel and the girl Grethel. He had little to bite and to break, and once when great scarcity fell on the land, he could no longer procure daily bread. Now when he thought over this by night in his bed, and tossed about in his anxiety, he groaned and said to his wife, 'What is to become of us? How are we to feed our poor children, when we no longer have anything even for ourselves?'

'I'll tell you what, husband,' answered the woman, 'Early tomorrow morning we will take the children out into the forest to where it is the thickest. There we will light a fire for them, and give each of them one piece of bread more, and then we will go to our work and leave them alone. They will not find the way home again, and we shall be rid of them.'

'No, wife,' said the man, 'I will not do that; how can I bear to leave my children alone in the forest? The wild animals would soon come and tear them to pieces.'

'O, thou fool!' said she, 'Then we must all four die of hunger, thou mayest as well plane the planks for our coffins,' and she left him no peace until he consented.

'But I feel very sorry for the poor children, all the same,' said the man.

The two children had also not been able to sleep for hunger, and had heard what their step-mother had said to their father. Grethel wept bitter tears, and said to Hansel, 'Now all is over with us.'

'Be quiet, Grethel,' said Hansel, 'do not distress thyself, I will soon find a way to help us.' And when the old folks had fallen asleep, he got up, put on his little coat, opened the door below, and crept outside. The moon shone brightly, and the white pebbles which lay in front of the house glittered like real silver pennies. Hansel stooped and put as many of them in the little pocket of his coat as he could possibly get in. Then he went back and said to Grethel, 'Be comforted, dear little sister, and sleep in peace, God will not forsake us,' and he lay down again in his bed.

When day dawned, but before the sun had risen, the woman came and awoke the two children, saying 'Get up, you sluggards! We are going into the forest to fetch wood.' She gave each a little piece of bread, and said, 'There is something for your dinner, but do not eat it up before then, for you will get nothing else.'

Grethel took the bread under her apron, as Hansel had the stones in his pocket. Then they all set out together on the way to the forest. When they had walked a short time, Hansel stood still and peeped back at the house, and did so again and again. His father said, 'Hansel, what art thou looking at there and staying behind for? Mind what thou art about, and do not forget how to use thy legs.'

'Ah, father,' said Hansel, 'I am looking at my little white cat, which is sitting up on the roof, and wants to say goodbye to me.'

The wife said, 'Fool, that is not thy little cat, that is the morning sun which is shining on the chimneys.' Hansel, however, had not been looking back at the cat, but had been constantly throwing one of the white pebble stones out of his pocket on the road.

When they had reached the middle of the forest, the father said, 'Now, children, pile up some wood, and I will light a fire that you may not be cold.' Hansel and Grethel gathered brushwood together, as high as a little hill. The brushwood was lighted, and when the flames were burning very high, the woman said, 'Now, children, lay yourselves down by the fire and rest, we will go into the forest and cut some wood. When we have done, we will come back and fetch you away.'

Hansel and Grethel sat by the fire, and when noon came, each ate a little piece of bread, and as they heard the strokes of the wood-axe they believed that their father was near. It was not, however, the axe, it was a branch which he had fastened to a withered tree which the wind was blowing backwards and forwards. And as they had been sitting such a long time, their eyes shut with fatigue, and they fell fast asleep. When at last they awoke, it was already dark night. Grethel began to cry and said, 'How are we to get out of the forest now?' But Hansel comforted her and said, 'Just wait a little, until the moon has risen, and then we will soon find the way.' And when the full moon had risen, Hansel took his little sister by the hand, and followed the pebbles, which shone like newly coined silver pieces, and showed them the way.

They walked the whole night long, and by break of day came once more to their father's house. They knocked at the door, and when the woman opened it and saw that it was Hansel and Grethel, she said, 'You naughty children, why have you slept so long in the forest? We thought you were never coming back at all!' The father, however, rejoiced, for it had cut him to the heart to leave them behind alone.

Not long afterwards, there was once more great scarcity in all parts, and the children heard their mother saying at night to their father, 'Everything is eaten again, we have one half loaf left, and after that there is an end. The children must go, we will take them farther into the wood, so that they will not find their way out again; there is no other means of saving ourselves!'

The man's heart was heavy, and he thought, 'It would be better for thee to share the last mouthful with thy children.' The woman, however, would listen to nothing that he had to say, but scolded and reproached him. He who says A must say B, likewise, and as he had yielded the first time, he had to do so a second time also.

The children were, however, still awake and had heard the conversation. When the old folks were asleep, Hansel again got up, and wanted to go out and pick up pebbles as he had done before, but the woman had locked the door, and Hansel could not get out. Nevertheless, he comforted his little sister, and said, 'Do not cry, Grethel, go to sleep quietly, the good God will help us.'

Early in the morning came the woman, and took the children out of their beds. Their bit of bread was given to them, but it was still smaller than the time before. On the way into the forest Hansel crumbled his in his pocket, and often stood still and threw a morsel on the ground. 'Hansel, why dost thou stop and look round?' said the father, 'go on.'

'I am looking back at my little pigeon which is sitting on the roof, and wants to say goodbye to me,' answered Hansel.

'Simpleton!' said the woman, 'that is not thy little pigeon, that is the morning sun that is shining on the chimney.'

Hansel, however, little by little, threw all the crumbs on the path.

The woman led the children still deeper into the forest, where they had never in their lives been before. Then a great fire was again made, and the mother said, 'Just sit there, you children, and when you are tired you may sleep a little; we are going into the forest to cut wood, and in the evening when we are done, we will come and fetch you away.'

When it was noon, Grethel shared her piece of bread with Hansel, who had scattered his by the way. Then they fell asleep and evening came and went, but no one came to the poor children. They did not awake until it was dark night, and Hansel comforted his little sister and said, 'Just wait, Grethel, until the moon rises, and then we shall see the crumbs of bread which I have strewn about, they will show us our way home again.'

When the moon came they set out, but they found no crumbs, for the many thousands of birds which fly about in the woods and fields had picked them all up. Hansel said to Grethel, 'We shall soon find the way,' but they did not find it. They walked the whole night and all the next day too from morning till evening, but they did not get out of the forest, and were very hungry, for they had nothing to eat but two or three berries, which grew on the ground. And as they were so weary that their legs would carry them no longer, they lay down beneath a tree and fell asleep.

It was now three mornings since they had left their father's house. They began to walk again, but they always got deeper into the forest, and if help did not come soon, they must die of hunger and weariness. When it was midday, they saw a beautiful snow-white bird sitting on a bough, which sang so delightfully that they stood still and listened to it. And when it had finished its song, it spread its wings and flew away before them, and they followed it until they reached a little house, on the roof of which it alighted; and when they came quite up to the little house they saw that it was built of bread and covered with cakes, but that the windows were of clear sugar. 'We will set to work on that,' said Hansel, 'and have a good meal. I will eat a bit of the roof, and thou, Grethel, canst eat some of the window, it will taste sweet.' Hansel reached up above, and broke off a little of the roof to try how it tasted, and Grethel leant against the window and nibbled at the panes. Then a soft voice cried from the room,

'Nibble, nibble, gnaw,
Who is nibbling at my little house?'

The children answered,

'The wind, the wind,
The heaven-born wind,'

and went on eating without disturbing themselves. Hansel, who thought the roof tasted very nice, tore down a great piece of it, and Grethel pushed out the whole of one round windowpane, sat down, and enjoyed herself with it. Suddenly, the door opened, and a very, very old woman, who supported herself on crutches, came creeping out. Hansel and Grethel were so terribly frightened that they let fall what they had in their hands.

The old woman, however, nodded her head, and said, 'Oh, you dear children, who has brought you here? Do come in, and stay with me. No harm shall happen to you.' She took them both by the hand, and led them into her little house. Then good food was set before them, milk and pancakes, with sugar, apples, and nuts. Afterwards two pretty little beds were covered with clean white linen, and Hansel and Grethel lay down in them, and thought they were in heaven.

The old woman had only pretended to be so kind; she was in reality a wicked witch, who lay in wait for children, and had only built the little house of bread in order to entice them there. When a child fell into her power, she killed it, cooked and ate it, and that was a feast day with her. Witches have red eyes, and cannot see far, but they have a keen scent like the beasts, and are aware when human beings draw near. When Hansel and Grethel came into her neighbourhood, she laughed maliciously, and said mockingly, 'I have them, they shall not escape me again!'

Early in the morning before the children were awake, she was already up, and when she saw both of them sleeping and looking so pretty, with their plump red cheeks, she muttered to herself, 'That will be a dainty mouthful!' Then she seized Hansel with her shrivelled hand, carried him into a little stable, and shut him in with a grated door. He might scream as he liked, that was of no use.

Then she went to Grethel, shook her till she awoke, and cried, 'Get up, lazy thing, fetch some water, and cook something good for thy brother, he is in the stable outside, and is to be made fat. When he is fat, I will eat him.' Grethel began to weep bitterly, but it was all in vain, she was forced to do what the wicked witch ordered her.

And now the best food was cooked for poor Hansel, but Grethel got nothing but crab shells. Every morning, the woman crept to the little stable, and cried, 'Hansel, stretch out thy finger that I may feel if thou wilt soon be fat.' Hansel, however, stretched out a little bone to her, and the old woman, who had dim eyes, could not see it, and thought it was Hansel's finger, and was astonished that there was no way of fattening him.

When four weeks had gone by, and Hansel still continued thin, she was seized with impatience and would not wait any longer. 'Hola, Grethel,' she cried to the girl, 'be active, and bring some water. Let Hansel be fat or lean, tomorrow I will kill him, and cook him.'

Ah, how the poor little sister did lament when she had to fetch the water, and how her tears did flow down over her cheeks! 'Dear God, do help us,' she cried. 'If the wild beasts in the forest had but devoured us, we should at any rate have died together.'

'Just keep thy noise to thyself,' said the old woman, 'all that won't help thee at all.'

Early in the morning, Grethel had to go out and hang up the cauldron with the water, and light the fire. 'We will bake first,' said the old woman, 'I have already heated the oven, and kneaded the dough.' She pushed poor Grethel out to the oven, from which flames of fire were already darting. 'Creep in,' said the witch, 'and see if it is properly heated, so that we can shut the bread in.' And when once Grethel was inside, she intended to shut the oven and let her bake in it, and then she would eat her, too. But Grethel saw what she had in her mind, and said, 'I do not know how I am to do it; how do you get in?'

'Silly goose,' said the old woman, 'The door is big enough; just look, I can get in myself!' And she crept up and thrust her head into the oven. Then Grethel gave her a push that drove her far into it, and shut the iron door, and fastened the bolt. Oh! then she began to howl quite horribly, but Grethel ran away, and the godless witch was miserably burnt to death.

Grethel, however, ran like lightning to Hansel, opened his little stable, and cried, 'Hansel, we are saved! The old witch is dead!'

Then Hansel sprang out like a bird from its cage when the door is opened for it. How they did rejoice and embrace each other, and dance about and kiss each other! And as they had no longer any need to fear her, they went into the witch's house, and in every corner there stood chests full of pearls and jewels. 'These are far better than pebbles!' said Hansel, and thrust into his pockets whatever could be got in, and Grethel said, 'I, too, will take something home with me,' and filled her pinafore full. 'But now we will go away,' said Hansel, 'that we may get out of the witch's forest.'

When they had walked for two hours, they came to a great piece of water. 'We cannot get over,' said Hansel, 'I see no foot-plank, and no bridge.'

'And no boat crosses either,' answered Grethel, 'but a white duck is swimming there; if I ask her, she will help us over.' Then she cried,

'Little duck, little duck, dost thou see,
Hansel and Grethel are waiting for thee?
There's never a plank, or bridge in sight,
Take us across on thy back so white.'

The duck came to them, and Hansel seated himself on its back, and told his sister to sit by him. 'No,' replied Grethel, 'that will be too heavy for the little duck; she shall take us across, one after the other.'

The good little duck did so, and when they were once safely across and had walked for a short time, the forest seemed to be more and more familiar to them, and at length they saw from afar their father's house. Then they began to run, rushed into the parlour, and threw themselves into their father's arms. The man had not known one happy hour since he had left the children in the forest; the woman, however, was dead. Grethel emptied her pinafore until pearls and precious stones ran about the room, and Hansel threw one handful after another out of his pocket to add to them. Then all anxiety was at an end, and they lived together in perfect happiness. My tale is done, there runs a mouse, whosoever catches it, may make himself a big fur cap out of it.

THE VALIANT LITTLE TAILOR

One summer's morning a little tailor was sitting on his table by the window; he was in good spirits, and sewed with all his might. Then came a peasant woman down the street crying, 'Good jams, cheap! Good jams, cheap!' This rang pleasantly in the tailor's ears; he stretched his delicate head out of the window, and called, 'Come up here, dear woman; here you will get rid of your goods.'

The woman came up the three steps to the tailor with her heavy basket, and he made her unpack the whole of the pots for him. He inspected all of them, lifted them up, put his nose to them, and at length said, 'The jam seems to me to be good, so weigh me out four ounces, dear woman, and if it is a quarter of a pound that is of no consequence.'

The woman who had hoped to find a good sale, gave him what he desired, but went away quite angry and grumbling.

'Now, God bless the jam to my use,' cried the little tailor, 'and give me health and strength.' So he brought the bread out of the cupboard, cut himself a piece right across the loaf and spread the jam over it. 'This won't taste bitter,' said he, 'but I will just finish the jacket before I take a bite.' He laid the bread near him, sewed on, and in his joy, made bigger and bigger stitches.

In the meantime, the smell of the sweet jam ascended so to the wall, where the flies were sitting in great numbers, that they were attracted and descended on it in hosts. 'Oi! Who invited you?' said the little tailor, and drove the unbidden guests away.

The flies, however, who understood no German, would not be turned away, but came back again in ever-increasing companies. The little tailor at last lost all patience, and got a bit of cloth from the hole under his worktable, and saying, 'Wait, and I will give it to you,' struck it mercilessly on them. When he drew it away and counted, there lay before him no fewer than seven, dead and with legs stretched out. 'Art thou a fellow of that sort?' said he, and could not help admiring his own bravery. 'The whole town shall know of this!' And the little tailor hastened to cut himself a girdle, stitched it, and embroidered on it in large letters, 'Seven at one stroke!'

'What, the town!' he continued, 'The whole world shall hear of it!' and his heart wagged with joy like a lamb's tail. The tailor put on the girdle, and resolved to go forth into the world, because he thought his workshop was too small for his valour. Before he went away, he sought about in the house to see if there was anything which he could take with him; however, he found nothing but an old cheese, and that he put in his pocket. In front of the door, he observed a bird which had caught itself in the thicket. It had to go into his pocket with the cheese. Now he took to the road boldly, and as he was light and nimble, he felt no fatigue.

The road led him up a mountain, and when he had reached the highest point of it, there sat a powerful giant looking about him quite comfortably. The little tailor went bravely up, spoke to him, and said, 'Good day, comrade, so thou art sitting there overlooking the wide-spread world! I am just on my way thither, and want to try my luck. Hast thou any inclination to go with me?'

The giant looked contemptuously at the tailor, and said, 'Thou ragamuffin! Thou miserable creature!'

'Oh, indeed?' answered the little tailor, and unbuttoned his coat, and showed the giant the girdle, 'There mayst thou read what kind of a man I am!' The giant read, 'Seven at one stroke,' and thought that they had been men whom the tailor had killed, and began to feel a little respect for the tiny fellow. Nevertheless, he wished to try him first, and took a stone in his hand and squeezed it together so that water dropped out of it. 'Do that likewise,' said the giant, 'if thou hast strength?'

'Is that all?' said the tailor, 'that is child's play with us!' and put his hand into his pocket, brought out the soft cheese, and pressed it until the liquid ran out of it. 'Faith,' said he, 'that was a little better, wasn't it?'

The giant did not know what to say, and could not believe it of the little man. Then the giant picked up a stone and threw it so high that the eye could scarcely follow it. 'Now, little mite of a man, do that likewise.'

'Well thrown,' said the tailor, 'but after all the stone came down to earth again; I will throw you one which shall never come back at all.' And he put his hand into his pocket, took out the bird, and threw it into the air. The bird, delighted with its liberty, rose, flew away and did not come back. 'How does that shot please you, comrade?' asked the tailor.

'Thou canst certainly throw,' said the giant, 'but now we will see if thou art able to carry anything properly.' He took the little tailor to a mighty oak tree which lay there felled on the ground, and said, 'If thou art strong enough, help me to carry the tree out of the forest.'

'Readily,' answered the little man; 'take thou the trunk on thy shoulders, and I will raise up the branches and twigs; after all, they are the heaviest.' The giant took the trunk on his shoulder, but the tailor seated himself on a branch, and the giant who could not look round, had to carry away the whole tree, and the little tailor into the bargain: he behind, was quite merry and happy, and whistled the song, 'Three tailors rode forth from the gate', as if carrying the tree were child's play. The giant, after he had dragged the heavy burden part of the way, could go no further, and cried, 'Hark you, I shall have to let the tree fall!'

The tailor sprang nimbly down, seized the tree with both arms as if he had been carrying it, and said to the giant, 'Thou art such a great fellow, and yet canst not even carry the tree!'

They went on together, and as they passed a cherry tree, the giant laid hold of the top of the tree where the ripest fruit was hanging, bent it down, gave it into the tailor's hand, and bade him eat. But the little tailor was much too weak to hold the tree, and when the giant let it go, it sprang back again, and the tailor was hurried into the air with it. When he had fallen down again without injury, the giant said, 'What is this? Hast thou not strength enough to hold the weak twig?'

'There is no lack of strength,' answered the little tailor. 'Dost thou think that could be anything to a man who has struck down seven at one blow? I leapt over the tree because the huntsmen are shooting down there in the thicket. Jump as I did, if thou canst do it.'

The giant made the attempt, but could not get over the tree, and remained hanging in the branches, so that in this also the tailor kept the upper hand.

The giant said, 'If thou art such a valiant fellow, come with me into our cavern and spend the night with us.' The little tailor was willing, and followed him. When they went into the cave, other giants were sitting there by the fire, and each of them had a roasted sheep in his hand and was eating it. The little tailor looked round and thought, 'It is much more spacious here than in my workshop.' The giant showed him a bed, and said he was to lie down in it and sleep. The bed, however, was too big for the little tailor; he did not lie down in it, but crept into a corner. When it was midnight, and the giant thought that the little tailor was lying in a sound sleep, he got up, took a great iron bar, cut through the bed with one blow, and thought he had given the grasshopper his finishing stroke. With the earliest dawn, the giants went into the forest and had quite forgotten the little tailor, when all at once he walked up to them quite merrily and boldly. The giants were terrified, they were afraid that he would strike them all dead, and ran away in a great hurry.

The little tailor went onwards, always following his own pointed nose. After he had walked for a long time, he came to the courtyard of a royal palace, and as he felt weary, he lay down on the grass and fell asleep. Whilst he lay there, the people came and inspected him on all sides, and read on his girdle, 'Seven at one stroke.'

'Ah,' said they, 'What does the great warrior here in the midst of peace? He must be a mighty lord.' They went and announced him to the King, and gave it as their opinion that if war should break out, this would be a weighty and useful man who ought on no account to be allowed to depart. The counsel pleased the King, and he sent one of his courtiers to the little tailor to offer him military service when he awoke. The ambassador remained standing by the sleeper, waited until he stretched his limbs and opened his eyes, and then conveyed to him this proposal. 'For this very reason have I come here,' the tailor replied, 'I am ready to enter the King's service.' He was therefore honourably received and a special dwelling was assigned him.

The soldiers, however, were set against the little tailor, and wished him a thousand miles away. 'What is to be the end of this?' they said amongst themselves. 'If we quarrel with him, and he strikes about him, seven of us will fall at every blow; not one of us can stand against him.' They came therefore to a decision, betook themselves in a body to the King, and begged for their dismissal. 'We are not prepared,' said they, 'to stay with a man who kills seven at one stroke.'

The King was sorry that for the sake of one he should lose all his faithful servants, wished that he had never set eyes on the tailor, and would willingly have been rid of him again. But he did not venture to give him his dismissal, for he dreaded lest he should strike him and all his people dead, and place himself on the royal throne. He thought about it for a long time, and at last found good counsel. He sent to the little tailor and caused him to be informed that as he was such a great warrior, he had one request to make to him. In a forest of his country lived two giants who caused great mischief with their robbing, murdering, ravaging and burning, and no one could approach them without putting himself in danger of death. If the tailor conquered and killed these two giants, he would give him his only daughter to wife, and half of his kingdom as a dowry, likewise one hundred horsemen should go with him to assist him.

'That would indeed be a fine thing for a man like me!' thought the little tailor. 'One is not offered a beautiful princess and half a kingdom every day of one's life!'

'Oh, yes,' he replied, 'I will soon subdue the giants, and do not require the help of the hundred horsemen to do it; he who can hit seven with one blow has no need to be afraid of two.'

The little tailor went forth, and the hundred horsemen followed him. When he came to the outskirts of the forest, he said to his followers, 'Just stay waiting here, I alone will soon finish off the giants.' Then he bounded into the forest and looked about right and left. After a while, he perceived both giants. They lay sleeping under a tree, and snored so that the branches waved up and down. The little tailor, not idle, gathered two pocketfuls of stones, and with these climbed up the tree. When he was halfway up, he slipped down by a branch, until he sat just above the sleepers, and then let one stone after another fall on the breast of one of the giants. For a long time the giant felt nothing, but at last he awoke, pushed his comrade, and said, 'Why art thou knocking me?'

'Thou must be dreaming,' said the other, 'I am not knocking thee.'

They laid themselves down to sleep again, and then the tailor threw a stone down on the second. 'What is the meaning of this?' cried the other. 'Why art thou pelting me?'

'I am not pelting thee,' answered the first, growling.

They disputed about it for a time, but as they were weary they let the matter rest, and their eyes closed once more. The little tailor began his game again, picked out the biggest stone, and threw it with all his might on the breast of the first giant. 'That is too bad!' cried he, and sprang up like a madman, and pushed his companion against the tree until it shook. The other paid him back in the same coin, and they got into such a rage that they tore up trees and belaboured each other so long, that at last they both fell down dead on the ground at the same time.

Then the little tailor leapt down. 'It is a lucky thing,' said he, 'that they did not tear up the tree on which I was sitting, or I should have had to spring on to another like a squirrel; but we tailors are nimble.'

He drew out his sword and gave each of them a couple of thrusts in the breast, and then went out to the horsemen and said, 'The work is done; I have given both of them their finishing stroke, but it was hard work! They tore up trees in their sore need, and defended themselves with them, but all that is to no purpose when a man like myself comes, who can kill seven at one blow.'

'But are you not wounded?' asked the horsemen.

'You need not concern yourself about that,' answered the tailor, 'They have not bent one hair of mine.'

The horsemen would not believe him, and rode into the forest; there they found the giants swimming in their blood, and all round about lay the torn-up trees.

The little tailor demanded of the King the promised reward; he, however, repented of his promise, and again bethought himself how he could get rid of the hero. 'Before thou receivest my daughter, and the half of my kingdom,' said he to him, 'thou must perform one more heroic deed. In the forest roams a unicorn which does great harm, and thou must catch it first.'

'I fear one unicorn still less than two giants. Seven at one blow, is my kind of affair.'

He took a rope and an axe with him, went forth into the forest, and again bade those who were sent with him to wait outside. He had to seek long. The unicorn soon came towards him, and rushed directly on the tailor, as if it would spit him on his horn without more ceremony. 'Softly, softly; it can't be done as quickly as that,' said he, and stood still and waited until the animal was quite close, and then sprang nimbly behind the tree. The unicorn ran against the tree with all its strength, and struck its horn so fast in the trunk that it had not strength enough to draw it out again, and thus it was caught.

'Now, I have got the bird,' said the tailor, and came out from behind the tree and put the rope round its neck, and then with his axe he hewed the horn out of the tree, and when all was ready he led the beast away and took it to the King.

The King still would not give him the promised reward, and made a third demand. Before the wedding, the tailor was to catch him a wild boar that made great havoc in the forest, and the huntsmen should give him their help.

'Willingly,' said the tailor, 'that is child's play!'

He did not take the huntsmen with him into the forest, and they were well pleased that he did not, for the wild boar had several times received them in such a manner that they had no inclination to lie in wait for him. When the boar perceived the tailor, it ran on him with foaming mouth and whetted tusks, and was about to throw him to the ground, but the active hero sprang into a chapel which was near, and up to the window at once, and in one bound out again. The boar ran in after him, but the tailor ran round outside and shut the door behind it, and then the raging beast, which was much too heavy and awkward to leap out of the window, was caught. The little tailor called the huntsmen thither that they might see the prisoner with their own eyes.

The hero, however went to the King, who was now, whether he liked it or not, obliged to keep his promise, and gave him his daughter and the half of his kingdom. Had he known that it was no warlike hero, but a little tailor who was standing before him, it would have gone to his heart still more than it did. The wedding was held with great magnificence and small joy, and out of a tailor a king was made.

After some time the young Queen heard her husband say in his dreams at night, 'Boy, make me the doublet, and patch the pantaloons, or else I will rap the yard-measure over thine ears.' Then she discovered in what state of life the young lord had been born, and next morning complained of her wrongs to her father, and begged him to help her to get rid of her husband, who was nothing else but a tailor.

The King comforted her and said, 'Leave thy bedroom door open this night, and my servants shall stand outside, and when he has fallen asleep shall go in, bind him, and take him on board a ship which shall carry him into the wide world.'

The woman was satisfied with this; but the King's armour-bearer, who had heard all, was friendly with the young lord, and informed him of the whole plot. 'I'll put a screw into that business,' said the little tailor.

At night he went to bed with his wife at the usual time, and when she thought that he had fallen asleep, she got up, opened the door, and then lay down again. The little tailor, who was only pretending to be asleep, began to cry out in a clear voice, 'Boy, make me the doublet and patch me the pantaloons, or I will rap the yard-measure over thine ears. I smote seven at one blow. I killed two giants, I brought away one unicorn and caught a wild boar, and am I to fear those who are standing outside the room?'

When these men heard the tailor speaking thus, they were overcome by a great dread, and ran as if the wild huntsman were behind them, and none of them would venture anything further against him. So the little tailor was a king and remained one, to the end of his life.

CINDERELLA

The wife of a rich man fell sick, and as she felt that her end was drawing near, she called her only daughter to her bedside and said, 'Dear child, be good and pious, and then the good God will always protect thee, and I will look down on thee from heaven and be near thee.' Thereupon she closed her eyes and departed. Every day the maiden went out to her mother's grave, and wept, and she remained pious and good. When winter came the snow spread a white sheet over the grave, and when the spring sun had drawn it off again, the man had taken another wife.

The woman had brought two daughters into the house with her, who were beautiful and fair of face, but vile and black of heart. Now began a bad time for the poor step-child. 'Is the stupid goose to sit in the parlour with us?' said they. 'He who wants to eat bread must earn it; out with the kitchen-wench.' They took her pretty clothes away from her, put an old grey bedgown on her, and gave her wooden shoes. 'Just look at the proud princess, how decked out she is!' they cried, and laughed, and led her into the kitchen. There she had to do hard work from morning till night, get up before daybreak, carry water, light fires, cook and wash. Besides this, the sisters did her every imaginable injury – they mocked her and emptied her peas and lentils into the ashes, so that she was forced to sit and pick them out again. In the evening when she had worked till she was weary, she had no bed to go to, but had to sleep by the fireside in the ashes. And as on that account she always looked dusty and dirty, they called her Cinderella. It happened that the father was once going to the fair, and he asked his two step-daughters what he should bring back for them. 'Beautiful dresses,' said one, 'Pearls and jewels,' said the second. 'And thou, Cinderella,' said he, 'what wilt thou have?'

'Father, break off for me the first branch which knocks against your hat on your way home.' So he bought beautiful dresses, pearls and jewels for his two step-daughters, and on his way home, as he was riding through a green thicket, a hazel twig brushed against him and knocked off his hat. Then he broke off the branch and took it with him. When he reached home he gave his step-daughters the things which they had wished for, and to Cinderella he gave the branch from the hazel-bush. Cinderella thanked him, went to her mother's grave and planted the branch on it, and wept so much that the tears fell down on it and watered it. And it grew, however, and became a handsome tree. Thrice a day Cinderella went and sat beneath it, and wept and prayed, and a little white bird always came on the tree, and if Cinderella expressed a wish, the bird threw down to her what she had wished for.

It happened, however, that the King appointed a festival which was to last three days, and to which all the beautiful young girls in the country were invited, in order that his son might choose himself a bride. When the two step-sisters heard that they too were to appear among the number, they were delighted, called Cinderella and said, 'Comb our hair for us, brush our shoes and fasten our buckles, for we are going to the festival at the King's palace.' Cinderella obeyed, but wept, because she too would have liked to go with them to the dance, and begged her step-mother to allow her to do so. 'Thou go, Cinderella!' said she; 'Thou art dusty and dirty and wouldst go to the festival? Thou hast no clothes and shoes, and yet wouldst dance!' As, however, Cinderella went on asking, the step-mother at last said, 'I have emptied a dish of lentils into the ashes for thee, if thou hast picked them out again in two hours, thou shalt go with us.' The maiden went through the back-door into the garden, and called, 'You tame pigeons, you turtle-doves, and all you birds beneath the sky, come and help me to pick

"The good into the pot,
The bad into the crop."'

Then two white pigeons came in by the kitchen-window, and afterwards the turtle-doves, and at last all the birds beneath the sky, came whirring and crowding in, and alighted amongst the ashes. And the pigeons nodded with their heads and began pick, pick, pick, pick, and the rest began also pick, pick, pick, pick, and gathered all the good grains into the dish. Hardly had one hour passed before they had finished, and all flew out again. Then the girl took the dish to her step-mother, and was glad, and believed that now she would be allowed to go with them to the festival. But the step-mother said, 'No, Cinderella, thou hast no clothes and thou canst not dance; thou wouldst only be laughed at.' And as Cinderella wept at this, the step-mother said, 'If thou canst pick two dishes of lentils out of the ashes for me in one hour, thou shalt go with us.' And she thought to herself, 'That she most certainly cannot do.' When the step-mother had emptied the two dishes of lentils amongst the ashes, the maiden went through the back-door into the garden and cried, 'You tame pigeons, you turtle-doves, and all you birds under heaven, come and help me to pick

"The good into the pot,

The bad into the crop.'"

Then two white pigeons came in by the kitchen-window, and afterwards the turtle-doves, and at length all the birds beneath the sky, came whirring and crowding in, and alighted amongst the ashes. And the doves nodded with their heads and began pick, pick, pick, pick, and the others began also pick, pick, pick, pick, and gathered all the good seeds into the dishes, and before half an hour was over they had already finished, and all flew out again. Then the maiden carried the dishes to the step-mother and was delighted, and believed that she might now go with them to the festival. But the step-mother said, 'All this will not help thee; thou goest not with us, for thou hast no clothes and canst not dance; we should be ashamed of thee!' On this she turned her back on Cinderella, and hurried away with her two proud daughters.

As no one was now at home, Cinderella went to her mother's grave beneath the hazel-tree, and cried,

'Shiver and quiver, little tree,
Silver and gold throw down over me.'

Then the bird threw a gold and silver dress down to her, and slippers embroidered with silk and silver. She put on the dress with all speed, and went to the festival. Her step-sisters and the step-mother, however, did not know her, and thought she must be a foreign princess, for she looked so beautiful in the golden dress. They never once thought of Cinderella, and believed that she was sitting at home in the dirt, picking lentils out of the ashes. The prince went to meet her, took her by the hand and danced with her. He would dance with no other maiden, and never left loose of her hand, and if any one else came to invite her, he said, 'This is my partner.'

She danced till it was evening, and then she wanted to go home. But the King's son said, 'I will go with thee and bear thee company,' for he wished to see to whom the beautiful maiden belonged. She escaped from him, however, and sprang into the pigeon-house. The King's son waited until her father came, and then he told him that the stranger maiden had leapt into the pigeon-house. The old man thought, 'Can it be Cinderella?' and they had to bring him an axe and a pickaxe that he might hew the pigeon-house to pieces, but no one was inside it. And when they got home Cinderella lay in her dirty clothes among the ashes, and a dim little oil-lamp was burning on the mantle-piece, for Cinderella had jumped quickly down from the back of the pigeon-house and had run to the little hazel-tree, and there she had taken off her beautiful clothes and laid them on the grave, and the bird had taken them away again, and then she had placed herself in the kitchen amongst the ashes in her grey gown.

Next day when the festival began afresh, and her parents and the step-sisters had gone once more, Cinderella went to the hazel-tree and said,

'Shiver and quiver, my little tree,
Silver and gold throw down over me.'

Then the bird threw down a much more beautiful dress than on the preceding day. And when Cinderella appeared at the festival in this dress, everyone was astonished at her beauty. The King's son had waited until she came, and instantly took her by the hand and danced with no one but her. When others came and invited her, he said, 'She is my partner.' When evening came she wished to leave, and the King's son followed her and wanted to see into which house she went. But she sprang away from him, and into the garden behind the house. Therein stood a beautiful tall tree on which hung the most magnificent pears. She clambered so nimbly between the branches like a squirrel that the King's son did not know where she was gone. He waited until her father came, and said to him, 'The stranger-maiden has escaped from me, and I believe she has climbed up the pear-tree.' The father thought, 'Can it be Cinderella?' and had an axe brought and cut the tree down, but no one was on it. And when they got into the kitchen, Cinderella lay there amongst the ashes, as usual, for she had jumped down on the other side of the tree, had taken the beautiful dress to the bird on the little hazel-tree, and put on her grey gown.

On the third day, when the parents and sisters had gone away, Cinderella went once more to her mother's grave and said to the little tree,

'Shiver and quiver, my little tree,
Silver and gold throw down over me.'

And now the bird threw down to her a dress which was more splendid and magnificent than any she had yet had, and the slippers were golden. And when she went to the festival in the dress, no one knew how to speak for astonishment. The King's son danced with her only, and if anyone invited her to dance, he said, 'She is my partner.'

When evening came, Cinderella wished to leave, and the King's son was anxious to go with her, but she escaped from him so quickly that he could not follow her. The King's son had, however, used a strategem, and had caused the whole staircase to be smeared with pitch, and there, when she ran down, had the maiden's left slipper remained sticking. The King's son picked it up, and it was small and dainty, and all golden. Next morning, he went with it to the father, and said to him, 'No one shall be my wife but she whose foot this golden slipper fits.' Then were the two sisters glad, for they had pretty feet. The eldest went with the shoe into her room and wanted to try it on, and her mother stood by. But she could not get her big toe into it, and the shoe was too small for her. Then her mother gave her a knife and said, 'Cut the toe off; when thou art Queen thou wilt have no more need to go on foot.' The maiden cut the toe off, forced the foot into the shoe, swallowed the pain, and went out to the King's son. Then he took her on his his horse as his bride and rode away with her. They were, however, obliged to pass the grave, and there, on the hazel-tree, sat the two pigeons and cried,

'Turn and peep, turn and peep,
There's blood within the shoe,
The shoe it is too small for her,
The true bride waits for you.'

Then he looked at her foot and saw how the blood was streaming from it. He turned his horse round and took the false bride home again, and said she was not the true one, and that the other sister was to put the shoe on. Then this one went into her chamber and got her toes safely into the shoe, but her heel was too large. So her mother gave her a knife and said, 'Cut a bit off thy heel; when thou art Queen thou wilt have no more need to go on foot.' The maiden cut a bit off her heel, forced her foot into the shoe, swallowed the pain, and went out to the King's son. He took her on his horse as his bride, and rode away with her, but when they passed by the hazel-tree, two little pigeons sat on it and cried,

> 'Turn and peep, turn and peep,
> There's blood within the shoe
> The shoe it is too small for her,
> The true bride waits for you.'

He looked down at her foot and saw how the blood was running out of her shoe, and how it had stained her white stocking. Then he turned his horse and took the false bride home again. 'This also is not the right one,' said he, 'have you no other daughter?'

'No,' said the man, 'There is still a little stunted kitchen-wench which my late wife left behind her, but she cannot possibly be the bride.' The King's son said he was to send her up to him; but the mother answered, 'Oh, no, she is much too dirty, she cannot show herself!' He absolutely insisted on it, and Cinderella had to be called. She first washed her hands and face clean, and then went and bowed down before the King's son, who gave her the golden shoe. Then she seated herself on a stool, drew her foot out of the heavy wooden shoe, and put it into the slipper, which fitted like a glove. And when she rose up and the King's son looked at her face he recognized the beautiful maiden who had danced with him and cried, 'That is the true bride!' The step-mother and the two sisters were terrified and became pale with rage; he, however, took Cinderella on his horse and rode away with her. As they passed by the hazel-tree, the two white doves cried:

> 'Turn and peep, turn and peep,
> No blood is in the shoe,
> The shoe is not too small for her,
> The true bride rides with you,'

and when they had cried that, the two came flying down and placed themselves on Cinderella's shoulders, one on the right, the other on the left, and remained sitting there.

When the wedding with the King's son had to be celebrated, the two false sisters came and wanted to get into favour with Cinderella and share her good fortune. When the betrothed couple went to church, the elder was at the right side and the younger at the left, and the pigeons pecked out one eye of each of them. Afterwards as they came back, the elder was at the left, and the younger at the right, and then the pigeons pecked out the other eye of each. And thus, for their wickedness and falsehood, they were punished with blindness as long as they lived.

THE MOUSE, THE BIRD AND THE SAUSAGE

Once on a time a mouse, a bird, and a sausage became companions, kept house together, lived well and happily with each other, and wonderfully increased their possessions. The bird's work was to fly every day into the forest and bring back wood. The mouse had to carry water, light the fire and lay the table, but the sausage had to cook.

He who is too well off is always longing for something new. One day, therefore, the bird met with another bird, on the way, to whom it related its excellent circumstances and boasted of them. The other bird, however, called it a poor simpleton for his hard work, but said that the two at home had good times. For when the mouse had made her fire and carried her water, she went into her little room to rest until they called her to lay the table. The sausage stayed by the pot, saw that the food was cooking well, and, when it was nearly time for dinner, it rolled itself once or twice through the broth or vegetables and then they were buttered, salted and ready. When the bird came home and laid his burden down, they sat down to dinner, and after they had had their meal, they slept their fill till next morning, and that was a splendid life.

Next day, the bird, prompted by the other bird, would go no more into the wood, saying that he had been servant long enough, and had been made a fool of by them, and that they must change about for once, and try to arrange it in another way. And, though the mouse and the sausage also begged most earnestly, the bird would have his way, and said it must be tried. They cast lots about it, and the lot fell on the sausage, who was to carry wood, the mouse became cook, and the bird was to fetch water.

What happened? The little sausage went out towards the wood, the little bird lit the fire, the mouse stayed by the pot and waited alone until little sausage came home and brought wood for next day. But the little sausage stayed so long on the road that they both feared something was amiss, and the bird flew out a little way in the air to meet it. Not far off, however, it met a dog on the road who had fallen on the poor sausage as lawful booty, and had seized and swallowed it. The bird charged the dog with an act of barefaced robbery, but it was in vain to speak, for the dog said he had found forged letters on the sausage, on which account its life was forfeited to him.

The bird sadly took up the wood, flew home, and related what he had seen and heard. They were much troubled, but agreed to do their best and remain together. The bird therefore laid the cloth, and the mouse made ready the food, and wanted to dress it, and to get into the pot as the sausage used to do, and roll and creep amongst the vegetables to mix them; but before she got into the midst of them she was stopped, and lost her skin and hair and life in the attempt.

When the bird came to carry up the dinner, no cook was there. In its distress the bird threw the wood here and there, called and searched, but no cook was to be found! Owing to his carelessness the wood caught fire, so that a conflagration ensued, the bird hastened to fetch water, and then the bucket dropped from his claws into the well, and he fell down with it, and could not recover himself, but had to drown there.

LITTLE RED-CAP[1]

Once upon a time there was a dear little girl who was loved by everyone who looked at her, but most of all by her grandmother, and there was nothing that she would not have given to the child. Once she gave her a little cap of red velvet, which suited her so well that she would never wear anything else; so she was always called 'Little Red-Cap'.

One day her mother said to her, 'Come, Little Red-Cap, here is a piece of cake and a bottle of wine; take them to your grandmother, she is ill and weak, and they will do her good. Set out before it gets hot, and when you are going, walk nicely and quietly and do not run off the path, or you may fall and break the bottle, and then your grandmother will get nothing; and when you go into her room, don't forget to say, "Good-morning", and don't peep into every corner before you do it.'

'I will take great care,' said Little Red-Cap to her mother, and gave her hand on it.

The grandmother lived out in the wood, half a league from the village, and just as Little Red-Cap entered the wood, a wolf met her. Red-Cap did not know what a wicked creature he was, and was not at all afraid of him.

'Good-day, Little Red-Cap,' said he.

'Thank you kindly, wolf.'

'Whither away so early, Little Red-Cap?'

'To my grandmother's.'

---

[1] The English version of this story, the well-known *Little Red-Riding-Hood*, is probably derived more immediately from the French, *Le Petit Chaperon Rouge*, as given by Perrault, where it ends with the death of the girl.

'What have you got in your apron?'

'Cake and wine; yesterday was baking-day, so poor sick grandmother is to have something good, to make her stronger.'

'Where does your grandmother live, Little Red-Cap?'

'A good quarter of a league farther on in the wood; her house stands under the three large oak-trees, the nut-trees are just below; you surely must know it,' replied Little Red-Cap.

The wolf thought to himself, 'What a tender young creature! what a nice plump mouthful – she will be better to eat than the old woman. I must act craftily, so as to catch both.' So he walked for a short time by the side of Little Red-Cap, and then he said, 'See Little Red-Cap, how pretty the flowers are about here – why do you not look round? I believe, too, that you do not hear how sweetly the little birds are singing; you walk gravely along as if you were going to school, while everything else out here in the wood is merry.'

Little Red-Cap raised her eyes, and when she saw the sunbeams dancing here and there through the trees, and pretty flowers growing everywhere, she thought, 'Suppose I take grandmother a fresh nosegay; that would please her too. It is so early in the day that I shall still get there in good time.' And so she ran from the path into the wood to look for flowers. And whenever she had picked one, she fancied that she saw a still prettier one farther on, and ran after it, and so got deeper and deeper into the wood.

Meanwhile, the wolf ran straight to the grandmother's house and knocked at the door.

'Who is there?'

'Little Red-Cap,' replied the wolf. 'She is bringing cake and wine; open the door.'

'Lift the latch,' called out the grandmother, 'I am too weak, and cannot get up.'

The wolf lifted the latch, the door flew open, and without saying a word he went straight to the grandmother's bed, and devoured her. Then he put on her clothes, dressed himself in her cap, laid himself in bed and drew the curtains.

Little Red-Cap, however, had been running about picking flowers, and when she had gathered so many that she could carry no more, she remembered her grandmother, and set out on the way to her.

She was surprised to find the cottage-door standing open, and when she went into the room, she had such a strange feeling that she said to herself, 'Oh dear! how uneasy I feel today, and at other times I like being with grandmother so much.' She called out, 'Good morning,' but received no answer; so she went to the bed and drew back the curtains. There lay her grandmother with her cap pulled far over her face, and looking very strange.

'Oh! grandmother,' she said, 'what big ears you have!'

'The better to hear you with, my child,' was the reply.

'But, grandmother, what big eyes you have!' she said.

'The better to see you with, my dear.'

'But, grandmother, what large hands you have!'

'The better to hug you with.'

'Oh! but, grandmother, what a terrible big mouth you have!'

'The better to eat you with!'

And scarcely had the wolf said this, than with one bound he was out of bed and swallowed up Red-Cap.

When the wolf had appeased his appetite, he lay down again in the bed, fell asleep and began to snore very loud. The huntsman was just passing the house, and thought to himself, 'How the old woman is snoring! I must just see if she wants anything.' So he went into the room, and when he came to the bed, he saw that the wolf was lying in it. 'Do I find thee here, thou old sinner!' said he. 'I have long sought thee!'

Then just as he was going to fire at him, it occurred to him that the wolf might have devoured the grandmother, and that she might still be saved, so he did not fire, but took a pair of scissors, and began to cut open the stomach of the sleeping wolf. When he had made two snips, he saw the little Red-Cap shining, and then he made two snips more, and the little girl sprang out, crying, 'Ah, how frightened I have been! How dark it was inside the wolf'; and after that the aged grandmother came out alive also, but scarcely able to breathe. Red-Cap, however, quickly fetched great stones with which they filled the wolf's body, and when he awoke, he wanted to run away, but the stones were so heavy that he fell down at once, and died.

Then all three were delighted. The huntsman drew off the wolf's skin and went home with it; the grandmother ate the cake and drank the wine which Red-Cap had brought, and revived, but Red-Cap thought to herself, 'As long as I live, I will never by myself leave the path, to run into the wood, when my mother has forbidden me to do so.'

It is also related that once when Red-Cap was again taking cakes to the old grandmother, another wolf spoke to her, and tried to entice her from the path. Red-Cap, however, was on her guard, and went straight forward on her way, and told her grandmother that she had met the wolf, and that he had said 'good morning' to her, but with such a wicked look in his eyes, that if they had not been on the public road she was certain he would have eaten her up. 'Well,' said the grandmother, 'we will shut the door, that he may not come in.'

Soon afterwards the wolf knocked, and cried, 'Open the door, grandmother, I am little Red-Cap, and am fetching you some cakes.' But they did not speak, or open the door, so the grey-beard stole twice or thrice round the house, and at last jumped on the roof, intending to wait until Red-Cap went home in the evening, and then to steal after her and devour her in the darkness. But the grandmother saw what was in his thoughts.

In front of the house was a great stone trough, so she said to the child, 'Take the pail, Red-Cap; I made some sausages yesterday, so carry the water in which I boiled them to the trough.' Red-Cap carried it until the great trough was quite full. Then the smell of the sausages reached the wolf, and he sniffed and peeped down, and at last stretched out his neck so far that he could no longer keep his footing and began to slip, and slipped down from the roof straight into the great trough, and was drowned. But Red-Cap went joyously home, and never did anything to harm anyone.

THE BREMEN TOWN-MUSICIANS

A certain man had a donkey, which had carried the corn-sacks to the mill indefatigably for many a long year; but his strength was going, and he was growing more and more unfit for work. Then his master began to consider how he might best save his keep; but the donkey, seeing that no good wind was blowing, ran away and set out on the road to Bremen. 'There,' he thought, 'I can surely be town-musician.' When he had walked some distance, he found a hound lying on the road, gasping like one who had run till he was tired. 'What are you gasping so for, you big fellow?' asked the donkey.

'Ah,' replied the hound, 'as I am old, and daily grow weaker, and no longer can hunt, my master wanted to kill me, so I took to flight; but now how am I to earn my bread?'

'I tell you what,' said the donkey, 'I am going to Bremen, and shall be town-musician there; go with me and engage yourself also as a musician. I will play the lute, and you shall beat the kettledrum.'

The hound agreed, and on they went.

Before long they came to a cat, sitting on the path, with a face like three rainy days! 'Now then, old shaver, what has gone askew with you?' asked the donkey.

'Who can be merry when his neck is in danger?' answered the cat. 'Because I am now getting old, and my teeth are worn to stumps, and I prefer to sit by the fire and spin, rather than hunt about after mice, my mistress wanted to drown me, so I ran away. But now good advice is scarce. Where am I to go?'

'Go with us to Bremen. You understand night-music, you can be a town-musician.'

The cat thought well of it, and went with them. After this the three fugitives came to a farmyard, where the cock was sitting upon the gate, crowing with all his might. 'Your crow goes through and through one,' said the donkey. 'What is the matter?'

'I have been foretelling fine weather, because it is the day on which Our Lady washes the Christ-child's little shirts, and wants to dry them,' said the cock; 'but guests are coming for Sunday, so the housewife has no pity, and has told the cook that she intends to eat me in the soup tomorrow, and this evening I am to have my head cut off. Now I am crowing at full pitch while I can.'

'Ah, but red-comb,' said the donkey, 'you had better come away with us. We are going to Bremen; you can find something better than death everywhere: you have a good voice, and if we make music together it must have some quality!'

The cock agreed to this plan, and all four went on together. They could not, however, reach the city of Bremen in one day, and in the evening they came to a forest where they meant to pass the night. The donkey and the hound laid themselves down under a large tree, the cat and the cock settled themselves in the branches; but the cock flew right to the top, where he was most safe. Before he went to sleep, he looked round on all four sides, and thought he saw in the distance a little spark burning; so he called out to his companions that there must be a house not far off, for he saw a light. The donkey said, 'If so, we had better get up and go on, for the shelter here is bad.' The hound thought that a few bones with some meat on would do him good too!

So they made their way to the place where the light was, and soon saw it shine brighter and grow larger, until they came to a well-lit robber's house. The donkey, as the biggest, went to the window and looked in.

'What do you see, my grey-horse?' asked the cock.

'What do I see?' answered the donkey; 'a table covered with good things to eat and drink, and robbers sitting at it enjoying themselves.'

'That would be the sort of thing for us,' said the cock.

'Yes, yes; ah, how I wish we were there!' said the donkey.

Then the animals took counsel together how they should manage to drive away the robbers, and at last they thought of a plan. The donkey was to place himself with his fore-feet upon the window-ledge, the hound was to jump on the donkey's back, the cat was to climb upon the dog, and lastly the cock was to fly up and perch upon the head of the cat.

When this was done, at a given signal, they began to perform their music together: the donkey brayed, the hound barked, the cat mewed, and the cock crowed; then they burst through the window into the room, so that the glass clattered! At this horrible din, the robbers sprang up, thinking no otherwise than that a ghost had come in, and fled in a great fright out into the forest. The four companions now sat down at the table, well content with what was left, and ate as if they were going to fast for a month.

As soon as the four minstrels had done, they put out the light, and each sought for himself a sleeping-place according to his nature and to what suited him. The donkey laid himself down upon some straw in the yard, the hound behind the door, the cat upon the hearth near the warm ashes, and the cock perched himself upon a beam of the roof; and being tired from their long walk, they soon went to sleep.

When it was past midnight, and the robbers saw from afar that the light was no longer burning in their house, and all appeared quiet, the captain said, 'We ought not to have let ourselves be frightened out of our wits'; and ordered one of them to go and examine the house.

The messenger finding all still, went into the kitchen to light a candle, and, taking the glistening fiery eyes of the cat for live coals, he held a lucifer-match to them to light it. But the cat did not understand the joke, and flew in his face, spitting and scratching. He was dreadfully frightened, and ran to the back door, but the dog, who lay there sprang up and bit his leg; and as he ran across the yard by the straw heap, the donkey gave him a smart kick with its hind foot. The cock, too, who had been awakened by the noise, and had become lively, cried down from the beam, 'Cock-a-doodle-doo!'

Then the robber ran back as fast as he could to his captain, and said, 'Ah, there is a horrible witch sitting in the house, who spat on me and scratched my face with her long claws, and by the door stands a man with a knife, who stabbed me in the leg; and in the yard there lies a black monster, who beat me with a wooden club; and above, upon the roof, sits the judge, who called out, "Bring the rogue here to me!", so I got away as well as I could.'

After this the robbers did not trust themselves in the house again; but it suited the four musicians of Bremen so well that they did not care to leave it any more. And the mouth of him who last told this story is still warm.

THE SINGING BONE

In a certain country, there was once great lamentation over a wild boar that laid waste the farmers' fields, killed the cattle, and ripped up people's bodies with his tusks. The King promised a large reward to anyone who would free the land from this plague; but the beast was so big and strong that no one dared to go near the forest in which it lived. At last, the King gave notice that whosoever should capture or kill the wild boar should have his only daughter to wife.

Now there lived in the country two brothers, sons of a poor man, who declared themselves willing to undertake the hazardous enterprise; the elder, who was crafty and shrewd, out of pride; the younger, who was innocent and simple, from a kind heart. The King said, 'In order that you may be the more sure of finding the beast, you must go into the forest from opposite sides.' So the elder went in on the west side, and the younger on the east.

When the younger had gone a short way, a little man stepped up to him. He held in his hand a black spear and said, 'I give you this spear because your heart is pure and good; with this you can boldly attack the wild boar, and it will do you no harm.'

He thanked the little man, shouldered the spear, and went on fearlessly.

Before long, he saw the beast, which rushed at him; but he held the spear towards it, and in its blind fury it ran so swiftly against it that its heart was cloven in twain. Then he took the monster on his back and went homewards with it to the King.

As he came out at the other side of the wood, there stood at the entrance a house where people were making merry with wine and dancing. His elder brother had gone in here, and, thinking that – after all – the boar would not run away from him, was going to drink until he felt brave. But when he saw his young brother coming out of the wood laden with his booty, his envious, evil heart gave him no peace. He called out to him, 'Come in, dear brother, rest and refresh yourself with a cup of wine.'

The youth, who suspected no evil, went in and told him about the good little man who had given him the spear wherewith he had slain the boar.

The elder brother kept him there until the evening, and then they went away together, and when in the darkness they came to a bridge over a brook, the elder brother let the other go first; and when he was halfway across he gave him such a blow from behind that he fell down dead. He buried him beneath the bridge, took the boar, and carried it to the King, pretending that he had killed it; whereupon he obtained the King's daughter in marriage. And when his younger brother did not come back he said, 'The boar must have killed him,' and every one believed it.

But as nothing remains hidden from God, so this black deed also was to come to light.

Years afterwards, a shepherd was driving his herd across the bridge, and saw lying in the sand beneath, a snow-white little bone. He thought that it would make a good mouth-piece, so he clambered down, picked it up, and cut out of it a mouth-piece for his horn. But when he blew through it for the first time, to his great astonishment, the bone began of its own accord to sing:

'Ah, friend, thou blowest upon my bone!
Long have I lain beside the water;
My brother slew me for the boar,
And took for his wife the King's young daughter.'

'What a wonderful horn!' said the shepherd; 'it sings by itself; I must take it to my lord the King.' And when he came with it to the King the horn again began to sing its little song. The King understood it all, and caused the ground below the bridge to be dug up, and then the whole skeleton of the murdered man came to light. The wicked brother could not deny the deed, and was sewn up in a sack and drowned. But the bones of the murdered man were laid to rest in a beautiful tomb in the churchyard.

THE DEVIL WITH THE THREE GOLDEN HAIRS

There was once a poor woman who gave birth to a little son; and as he came into the world with a caul on, it was predicted that in his fourteenth year he would have the King's daughter for his wife. It happened that soon afterwards the King came into the village, and no one knew that he was the King, and when he asked the people what news there was, they answered, 'A child has just been born with a caul on; whatever anyone so born undertakes turns out well. It is prophesied, too, that in his fourteenth year he will have the King's daughter for his wife.'

The King, who had a bad heart, and was angry about the prophecy, went to the parents, and, seeming quite friendly, said, 'You poor people, let me have your child, and I will take care of it.' At first, they refused, but when the stranger offered them a large amount of gold for it, and they thought, 'It is a luck-child, and everything must turn out well for it,' they at last consented, and gave him the child.

The King put it in a box and rode away with it until he came to a deep piece of water; then he threw the box into it and thought, 'I have freed my daughter from her unlooked-for suitor.'

The box, however, did not sink, but floated like a boat, and not a drop of water made its way into it. And it floated to within two miles of the King's chief city, where there was a mill, and it came to a standstill at the mill dam. A miller's boy, who by good luck was standing there, noticed it and pulled it out with a hook, thinking that he had found a great treasure, but when he opened it there lay a pretty boy inside, quite fresh and lively. He took him to the miller and his wife, and as they had no children they were glad, and said, 'God has given him to us.' They took great care of the foundling, and he grew up in all goodness.

It happened that once in a storm, the King went into the mill, and he asked the mill folk if the tall youth was their son. 'No,' answered they, 'he's a foundling. Fourteen years ago he floated down to the mill dam in a box, and the mill-boy pulled him out of the water.'

Then the King knew that it was none other than the luck-child, which he had thrown into the water, and he said, 'My good people, could not the youth take a letter to the Queen; I will give him two gold pieces as a reward?'

'Just as the King commands,' answered they, and they told the boy to hold himself in readiness. Then the King wrote a letter to the Queen, wherein he said, 'As soon as the boy arrives with this letter, let him be killed and buried, and all must be done before I come home.'

The boy set out with this letter; but he lost his way, and in the evening came to a large forest. In the darkness, he saw a small light; he went towards it and reached a cottage. When he went in, an old woman was sitting by the fire quite alone. She started when she saw the boy, and said, 'Whence do you come, and whither are you going?'

'I come from the mill,' he answered, 'and wish to go to the Queen, to whom I am taking a letter; but as I have lost my way in the forest I should like to stay here over night.'

'You poor boy,' said the woman, 'you have come into a den of thieves, and when they come home they will kill you.'

'Let them come,' said the boy, 'I am not afraid; but I am so tired that I cannot go any farther': and he stretched himself upon a bench and fell asleep.

Soon afterwards the robbers came, and angrily asked what strange boy was lying there? 'Ah,' said the old woman, 'it is an innocent child who has lost himself in the forest, and out of pity I have let him come in; he has to take a letter to the Queen.' The robbers opened the letter and read it, and in it was written that the boy as soon as he arrived should be put to death. Then the hard-hearted robbers felt pity, and their leader tore up the letter and wrote another, saying, that as soon as the boy came, he should be married at once to the King's daughter. Then they let him lie quietly on the bench until the next morning, and when he awoke they gave him the letter, and showed him the right way.

And the Queen, when she had received the letter and read it, did as was written in it, and had a splendid wedding feast prepared, and the King's daughter was married to the luck-child, and as the youth was handsome and agreeable she lived with him in joy and contentment.

After some time the King returned to his palace and saw that the prophecy was fulfilled, and the luck-child married to his daughter. 'How has that come to pass?' said he; 'I gave quite another order in my letter.'

So the Queen gave him the letter, and said that he might see for himself what was written in it. The King read the letter and saw quite well that it had been exchanged for the other. He asked the youth what had become of the letter entrusted to him, and why he had brought another instead of it. 'I know nothing about it,' answered he; 'it must have been changed in the night, when I slept in the forest.' The King said in a passion, 'You shall not have everything quite so much your own way; whosoever marries my daughter must fetch me from hell three golden hairs from the head of the devil; bring me what I want, and you shall keep my daughter.' In this way the King hoped to be rid of him forever. But the luck-child answered, 'I will fetch the golden hairs, I am not afraid of the Devil'; thereupon he took leave of them and began his journey.

The road led him to a large town, where the watchman by the gates asked him what his trade was, and what he knew. 'I know everything,' answered the luck-child. 'Then you can do us a favour,' said the watchman, 'if you will tell us why our market fountain, which once flowed with wine has become dry, and no longer gives even water?'

'That you shall know,' answered he; 'only wait until I come back.'

Then he went farther and came to another town, and there also the gatekeeper asked him what was his trade, and what he knew. 'I know everything,' answered he. 'Then you can do us a favour and tell us why a tree in our town which once bore golden apples now does not even put forth leaves?'

'You shall know that,' answered he; 'only wait until I come back.'

Then he went on and came to a wide river over which he must go. The ferryman asked him what his trade was, and what he knew. 'I know everything,' answered he. 'Then you can do me a favour,' said the ferryman, 'and tell me why I must always be rowing backwards and forwards, and am never set free?'

'You shall know that,' answered he; 'only wait until I come back.'

When he had crossed the water he found the entrance to Hell.

It was black and sooty within, and the Devil was not at home, but his grandmother was sitting in a large armchair. 'What do you want?' said she to him, but she did not look so very wicked. 'I should like to have three golden hairs from the devil's head,' answered he, 'else I cannot keep my wife.'

'That is a good deal to ask for,' said she; 'if the devil comes home and finds you, it will cost you your life; but as I pity you, I will see if I cannot help you.'

She changed him into an ant and said, 'Creep into the folds of my dress, you will be safe there.'

'Yes,' answered he, 'so far, so good; but there are three things besides that I want to know: why a fountain which once flowed with wine has become dry, and no longer gives even water; why a tree which once bore golden apples does not even put forth leaves; and why a ferryman must always be going backwards and forwards, and is never set free?'

'Those are difficult questions,' answered she, 'but only be silent and quiet and pay attention to what the devil says when I pull out the three golden hairs.'

As the evening came on, the devil returned home. No sooner had he entered than he noticed that the air was not pure. 'I smell man's flesh,' said he; 'all is not right here.'

Then he pried into every corner, and searched, but could not find anything. His grandmother scolded him. 'It has just been swept,' said she, 'and everything put in order, and now you are upsetting it again; you have always got man's flesh in your nose. Sit down and eat your supper.'

When he had eaten and drunk, he was tired, and laid his head in his grandmother's lap, and before long he was fast asleep, snoring and breathing heavily. Then the old woman took hold of a golden hair, pulled it out, and laid it down near her. 'Oh!' cried the devil, 'what are you doing?'

'I have had a bad dream,' answered the grandmother, 'so I seized hold of your hair.'

'What did you dream then?' said the devil.

'I dreamed that a fountain in a market-place from which wine once flowed was dried up, and not even water would flow out of it; what is the cause of it?'

'Oh, ho! if they did but know it,' answered the devil; 'there is a toad sitting under a stone in the well; if they killed it, the wine would flow again.'

He went to sleep again and snored until the windows shook. Then she pulled the second hair out. 'Ha! what are you doing?' cried the devil angrily.

'Do not take it ill,' said she, 'I did it in a dream.'

'What have you dreamt this time?' asked he.

'I dreamt that in a certain kingdom there stood an apple tree which had once borne golden apples, but now would not even bear leaves. What, think you, was the reason?'

'Oh! If they did but know,' answered the devil. 'A mouse is gnawing at the root; if they killed this they would have golden apples again, but if it gnaws much longer the tree will wither altogether. But leave me alone with your dreams: if you disturb me in my sleep again you will get a box on the ear.'

The grandmother spoke gently to him until he fell asleep again and snored. Then she took hold of the third golden hair and pulled it out. The devil jumped up, roared out, and would have treated her ill if she had not quieted him once more and said, 'Who can help bad dreams?'

'What was the dream, then?' asked he, and was quite curious.

'I dreamt of a ferryman who complained that he must always ferry from one side to the other, and was never released. What is the cause of it?'

'Ah! the fool,' answered the devil; 'when anyone comes and wants to go across he must put the oar in his hand, and the other man will have to ferry and he will be free.' As the grandmother had plucked out the three golden hairs, and the three questions were answered, she let the old serpent alone, and he slept until daybreak.

When the devil had gone out again the old woman took the ant out of the folds of her dress, and gave the luck-child his human shape again. 'There are the three golden hairs for you,' said she. 'What the Devil said to your three questions, I suppose you heard?'

'Yes,' answered he, 'I heard, and will take care to remember.'

'You have what you want,' said she, 'and now you can go your way.'

He thanked the old woman for helping him in his need, and left hell well content that everything had turned out so fortunately.

When he came to the ferryman he was expected to give the promised answer.

'Ferry me across first,' said the luck-child, 'and then I will tell you how you can be set free,' and when he reached the opposite shore he gave him the devil's advice: 'Next time anyone comes, who wants to be ferried over, just put the oar in his hand.'

He went on and came to the town wherein stood the unfruitful tree, and there too the watchman wanted an answer. So he told him what he had heard from the devil: 'Kill the mouse which is gnawing at its root, and it will again bear golden apples.' Then the watchman thanked him, and gave him as a reward two asses laden with gold, which followed him.

THE DEVIL WITH THE THREE GOLDEN HAIRS

At last he came to the town whose well was dry. He told the watchman what the devil had said: 'A toad is in the well beneath a stone; you must find it and kill it, and the well will again give wine in plenty.' The watchman thanked him, and also gave him two asses laden with gold.

At last the luck-child got home to his wife, who was heartily glad to see him again, and to hear how well he had prospered in everything. To the King, he took what he had asked for, the devil's three golden hairs, and when the King saw the four asses laden with gold he was quite content, and said, 'Now all the conditions are fulfilled, and you can keep my daughter. But tell me, dear son-in-law, where did all that gold come from? This is tremendous wealth!'

'I was rowed across a river,' answered he, 'and got it there; it lies on the shore instead of sand.'

'Can I too fetch some of it?' said the King; and he was quite eager about it.

'As much as you like,' answered he. 'There is a ferryman on the river; let him ferry you over, and you can fill your sacks on the other side.'

The greedy King set out in all haste, and when he came to the river he beckoned to the ferryman to put him across. The ferryman came and bade him get in, and when they got to the other shore he put the oar in his hand and sprang out. But from this time forth the King had to ferry, as a punishment for his sins. Perhaps he is ferrying still? If he is, it is because no one has taken the oar from him.

THE ELVES

FIRST STORY

A shoemaker, by no fault of his own, had become so poor that at last he had nothing left but leather for one pair of shoes. So in the evening, he cut out the shoes which he wished to begin to make the next morning, and as he had a good conscience, he lay down quietly in his bed, commended himself to God, and fell asleep.

In the morning, after he had said his prayers, and was just going to sit down to work, the two shoes stood quite finished on his table. He was astounded, and knew not what to say to it. He took the shoes in his hands to observe them closer, and they were so neatly made that there was not one bad stitch in them, just as if they were intended as a masterpiece. Soon after, a buyer came in, and as the shoes pleased him so well, he paid more for them than was customary, and, with the money, the shoemaker was able to purchase leather for two pairs of shoes. He cut them out at night, and next morning was about to set to work with fresh courage; but he had no need to do so, for, when he got up, they were already made, and buyers also were not wanting, who gave him money enough to buy leather for four pairs of shoes. The following morning, too, he found the four pairs made; and so it went on constantly, what he cut out in the evening was finished by the morning, so that he soon had his honest independence again, and at last became a wealthy man.

Now it befell that one evening not long before Christmas, when the man had been cutting out, he said to his wife, before going to bed, 'What think you if we were to stay up tonight to see who it is that lends us this helping hand?' The woman liked the idea, and lit a candle, and then they hid themselves in a corner of the room, behind some clothes which were hanging up there, and watched. When it was midnight, two pretty little naked men came, sat down by the shoemaker's table, took all the work which was cut out before them and began to stitch, and sew, and hammer so skilfully and so quickly with their little fingers that the shoemaker could not turn away his eyes for astonishment. They did not stop until all was done, and stood finished on the table, and they ran quickly away.

Next morning the woman said, 'The little men have made us rich, and we really must show that we are grateful for it. They run about so, and have nothing on, and must be cold. I'll tell thee what I'll do: I will make them little shirts, and coats, and vests, and trousers, and knit both of them a pair of stockings, and do thou, too, make them two little pairs of shoes.' The man said, 'I shall be very glad to do it'; and one night, when everything was ready, they laid their presents all together on the table instead of the cut-out work, and then concealed themselves to see how the little men would behave.

At midnight, they came bounding in, and wanted to get to work at once, but as they did not find any leather cut out, but only the pretty little articles of clothing, they were at first astonished, and then they showed intense delight. They dressed themselves with the greatest rapidity, putting the pretty clothes on, and singing,

'Now we are boys so fine to see,

Why should we longer cobblers be?'

Then they danced and skipped and leapt over chairs and benches. At last they danced out of doors. From that time forth they came no more, but as long as the shoemaker lived all went well with him, and all his undertakings prospered.

SECOND STORY

There was once a poor servant-girl, who was industrious and cleanly, and swept the house every day, and emptied her sweepings on the great heap in front of the door. One morning when she was just going back to her work, she found a letter on this heap, and as she could not read, she put her broom in the corner, and took the letter to her master and mistress, and behold it was an invitation from the elves, who asked the girl to hold a child for them at its christening. The girl did not know what to do, but at length, after much persuasion, and as they told her that it was not right to refuse an invitation of this kind, she consented. Then three elves came and conducted her to a hollow mountain, where the little folks lived.

Everything there was small, but more elegant and beautiful than can be described. The baby's mother lay in a bed of black ebony ornamented with pearls, the coverlets were embroidered with gold, the cradle was of ivory, the bath of gold. The girl stood as godmother, and then wanted to go home again, but the little elves urgently entreated her to stay three days with them. So she stayed, and passed the time in pleasure and gaiety, and the little folks did all they could to make her happy.

At last she set out on her way home. Then first they filled her pockets quite full of money, and after that they led her out of the mountain again. When she got home, she wanted to begin her work, and took the broom, which was still standing in the corner, in her hand and began to sweep. Then some strangers came out of the house, who asked her who she was, and what business she had there? And she had not, as she thought, been three days with the little men in the mountains, but seven years, and in the meantime her former masters had died.

THIRD STORY

A certain mother's child had been taken away out of its cradle by the elves, and a changeling with a large head and staring eyes, which would do nothing but eat and drink, laid in its place. In her trouble, she went to her neighbour, and asked her advice. The neighbour said that she was to carry the changeling into the kitchen, set it down on the hearth, light a fire, and boil some water in two egg shells, which would make the changeling laugh, and if he laughed, all would be over with him.

The woman did everything that her neighbour bade her. When she put the egg shells with water on the fire, the imp said, 'I am as old now as the Wester forest, but never yet have I seen any one boil anything in an egg shell!' And he began to laugh at it. Whilst he was laughing, suddenly came a host of little elves, who brought the right child, set it down on the hearth, and took the changeling away with them.

THE ROBBER BRIDEGROOM

There was once on a time a miller, who had a beautiful daughter, and as she was grown up, he wished that she was provided for, and well married. He thought, 'If any good suitor comes and asks for her, I will give her to him.' Not long afterwards, a suitor came, who appeared to be very rich, and as the miller had no fault to find with him, he promised his daughter to him.

The maiden, however, did not like him quite so much as a girl should like the man to whom she is engaged, and had no confidence in him. Whenever she saw, or thought of him, she felt a secret horror. Once he said to her, 'Thou art my betrothed, and yet thou hast never once paid me a visit.' The maiden replied, 'I know not where thy house is.' Then said the bridegroom, 'My house is out there in the dark forest.' She tried to excuse herself and said she could not find the way there. The bridegroom said, 'Next Sunday thou must come out there to me; I have already invited the guests, and I will strew ashes in order that thou mayst find thy way through the forest.'

When Sunday came, and the maiden had to set out on her way, she became very uneasy, she herself knew not exactly why, and to mark her way she filled both her pockets full of peas and lentils. Ashes were strewn at the entrance of the forest, and these she followed, but at every step she threw a couple of peas on the ground. She walked almost the whole day until she reached the middle of the forest, where it was the darkest, and there stood a solitary house, which she did not like, for it looked so dark and dismal. She went inside it, but no one was within, and the most absolute stillness reigned. Suddenly a voice cried,

'Turn back, turn back, young maiden dear,
'Tis a murderer's house you enter here.'

The maiden looked up, and saw that the voice came from a bird, which was hanging in a cage on the wall. Again it cried,

'Turn back, turn back, young maiden dear,
'Tis a murderer's house you enter here.'

Then the young maiden went on farther from one room to another, and walked through the whole house, but it was entirely empty and not one human being was to be found. At last she came to the cellar, and there sat an extremely aged woman, whose head shook constantly. 'Can you not tell me,' said the maiden, 'if my betrothed lives here?'

'Alas, poor child,' replied the old woman, 'whither hast thou come? Thou art in a murderers' den. Thou thinkest thou art a bride soon to be married, but thou wilt keep thy wedding with death. Look, I have been forced to put a great kettle on there, with water in it, and when they have thee in their power, they will cut thee to pieces without mercy, will cook thee, and eat thee, for they are eaters of human flesh. If I do not have compassion on thee, and save thee, thou art lost.'

Thereupon the old woman led her behind a great hogshead where she could not be seen. 'Be as still as a mouse,' said she, 'do not make a sound, or move, or all will be over with thee. At night, when the robbers are asleep, we will escape; I have long waited for an opportunity.'

Hardly was this done, than the godless crew came home. They dragged with them another young girl. They were drunk, and paid no heed to her screams and lamentations. They gave her wine to drink, three glasses full, one glass of white wine, one glass of red, and a glass of yellow, and with this her heart burst in twain. Thereupon, they tore off her delicate raiment, laid her on a table, cut her beautiful body in pieces and strewed salt thereon. The poor bride behind the cask trembled and shook, for she saw right well what fate the robbers had destined for her. One of them noticed a gold ring on the little finger of the murdered girl, and as it would not come off at once, he took an axe and cut the finger off, but it sprang up in the air, away over the cask and fell straight into the bride's bosom. The robber took a candle and wanted to look for it, but could not find it. Then another of them said, 'Hast thou looked behind the great hogshead?' But the old woman cried, 'Come and get something to eat, and leave off looking till the morning, the finger won't run away from you.'

Then the robbers said, 'The old woman is right,' and gave up their search, and sat down to eat, and the old woman poured a sleeping-draught in their wine, so that they soon lay down in the cellar, and slept and snored. When the bride heard that, she came out from behind the hogshead, and had to step over the sleepers, for they lay in rows on the ground, and great was her terror lest she should waken one of them. But God helped her, and she got safely over. The old woman went up with her, opened the doors, and they hurried out of the murderers' den with all the speed in their power. The wind had blown away the strewn ashes, but the peas and lentils had sprouted and grown up, and showed them the way in the moonlight. They walked the whole night, until in the morning they arrived at the mill, and then the maiden told her father everything exactly as it had happened.

When the day came when the wedding was to be celebrated, the bridegroom appeared, and the Miller had invited all his relations and friends. As they sat at table, each was bidden to relate something. The bride sat still, and said nothing. Then said the bridegroom to the bride, 'Come, my darling, dost thou know nothing? Relate something to us like the rest.' She replied, 'Then I will relate a dream. I was walking alone through a wood, and at last I came to a house, in which no living soul was, but on the wall there was a bird in a cage which cried,

"Turn back, turn back, young maiden dear,
'Tis a murderer's house you enter here."

And this it cried once more. My darling, I only dreamt this. Then I went through all the rooms, and they were all empty, and there was something so horrible about them! At last I went down into the cellar, and there sat a very very old woman, whose head shook; I asked her, "Does my bridegroom live in this house?" She answered, "Alas poor child, thou hast got into a murderers' den, thy bridegroom does live here, but he will hew thee in pieces, and kill thee, and then he will cook thee, and eat thee." My darling, I only dreamt this. But the old woman hid me behind a great hogshead, and, scarcely was I hidden, when the robbers came home, dragging a maiden with them, to whom they gave three kinds of wine to drink, white, red, and yellow, with which her heart broke in twain. My darling, I only dreamt this. Thereupon, they pulled off her pretty clothes, and hewed her fair body in pieces on a table, and sprinkled them with salt. My darling, I only dreamt this. And one of the robbers saw that there was still a ring on her little finger, and as it was hard to draw off, he took an axe and cut it off, but the finger sprang up in the air, and sprang behind the great hogshead, and fell in my bosom. And there is the finger with the ring!' And with these words she drew it forth, and showed it to those present.

The robber, who had during this story become as pale as ashes, leapt up and wanted to escape, but the guests held him fast, and delivered him over to justice. Then he and his whole troop were executed for their infamous deeds.

OLD SULTAN

A farmer once had a faithful dog called Sultan, who had grown old, and lost all his teeth, so that he could no longer hold anything fast. One day, the farmer was standing with his wife before the house door, and said, 'Tomorrow I intend to shoot Old Sultan, he is no longer of any use.'

His wife, who felt pity for the faithful beast, answered, 'He has served us so long, and been so faithful, that we might well give him his keep.'

'Eh! what?' said the man. 'You are not very sharp. He has not a tooth left in his mouth, and not a thief is afraid of him; now he may be off. If he has served us, he has had good feeding for it.'

The poor dog, who was lying stretched out in the sun not far off, had heard everything, and was sorry that the morrow was to be his last day. He had a good friend, the wolf, and he crept out in the evening into the forest to him, and complained of the fate that awaited him. 'Hark ye, gossip,' said the wolf, 'be of good cheer, I will help you out of your trouble. I have thought of something. Tomorrow, early in the morning, your master is going with his wife to make hay, and they will take their little child with them, for no one will be left behind in the house. They are wont, during work-time, to lay the child under the hedge in the shade; you lay yourself there too, just as if you wished to guard it. Then I will come out of the wood, and carry off the child. You must rush swiftly after me, as if you would seize it again from me. I will let it fall, and you will take it back to its parents, who will think that you have saved it, and will be far too grateful to do you any harm; on the contrary, you will be in high favour, and they will never let you want for anything again.'

The plan pleased the dog, and it was carried out just as it was arranged. The father screamed when he saw the Wolf running across the field with his child, but when Old Sultan brought it back, then he was full of joy, and stroked him and said, 'Not a hair of yours shall be hurt, you shall eat my bread free as long as you live.' And to his wife he said, 'Go home at once and make Old Sultan some bread-sop that he will not have to bite, and bring the pillow out of my bed, I will give him that to lie upon.'

Henceforth Old Sultan was as well off as he could wish to be.

Soon afterwards the wolf visited him, and was pleased that everything had succeeded so well. 'But, gossip,' said he, 'you will just wink an eye if when I have a chance, I carry off one of your master's fat sheep.'

'Do not reckon upon that,' answered the dog; 'I will remain true to my master; I cannot agree to that.' The wolf, who thought that this could not be spoken in earnest, came creeping about in the night and was going to take away the sheep. But the farmer, to whom the faithful Sultan had told the wolf's plan, caught him and dressed his hide soundly with the flail. The wolf had to pack off, but he cried out to the dog, 'Wait a bit, you scoundrel, you shall pay for this.'

The next morning the wolf sent the boar to challenge the dog to come out into the forest so that they might settle the affair. Old Sultan could find no one to stand by him but a cat with only three legs, and as they went out together the poor cat limped along, and at the same time stretched out her tail into the air with pain.

The wolf and his friend were already on the spot appointed, but when they saw their enemy coming they thought that he was bringing a sabre with him, for they mistook the outstretched tail of the cat for one. And when the poor beast hopped on its three legs, they could only think every time that it was picking up a stone to throw at them. So they were both afraid; the wild boar crept into the underwood and the wolf jumped up a tree.

The dog and the cat, when they came up, wondered that there was no one to be seen. The wild boar, however, had not been able to hide himself altogether; and one of his ears was still to be seen. Whilst the cat was looking carefully about, the boar moved his ear; the cat, who thought it was a mouse moving there, jumped upon it and bit it hard. The boar made a fearful noise and ran away, crying out, 'The guilty one is up in the tree.' The dog and cat looked up and saw the wolf, who was ashamed of having shown himself so timid, and made friends with the dog.

THE SIX SWANS

Once upon a time, a certain King was hunting in a great forest, and he chased a wild beast so eagerly that none of his attendants could follow him. When evening drew near, he stopped and looked around him, and then he saw that he had lost his way. He sought a way out, but could find none. Then he perceived an aged woman with a head, which nodded perpetually, who came towards him, but she was a witch. 'Good woman,' said he to her, 'can you not show me the way through the forest?'

'Oh, yes, Lord King,' she answered, 'that I certainly can, but on one condition, and if you do not fulfil that, you will never get out of the forest, and will die of hunger in it.'

'What kind of condition is it?' asked the King.

'I have a daughter,' said the old woman, 'who is as beautiful as anyone in the world, and well deserves to be your consort, and if you will make her your Queen, I will show you the way out of the forest.'

In the anguish of his heart the King consented, and the old woman led him to her little hut, where her daughter was sitting by the fire. She received the King as if she had been expecting him, and he saw that she was very beautiful, but still she did not please him, and he could not look at her without secret horror. After he had taken the maiden up on his horse, the old woman showed him the way, and the King reached his royal palace again, where the wedding was celebrated.

The King had already been married once, and had by his first wife, seven children, six boys and a girl, whom he loved better than anything else in the world. As he now feared that the stepmother might not treat them well, and even do them some injury, he took them to a lonely castle which stood in the midst of a forest. It lay so concealed, and the way was so difficult to find that he himself would not have found it, if a wise woman had not given him a ball of yarn with wonderful properties. When he threw it down before him, it unrolled itself and showed him his path.

The King, however, went so frequently away to his dear children that the Queen observed his absence; she was curious and wanted to know what he did when he was quite alone in the forest. She gave a great deal of money to his servants, and they betrayed the secret to her, and told her likewise of the ball which alone could point out the way. And now she knew no rest until she had learnt where the King kept the ball of yarn, and then she made little shirts of white silk, and as she had learnt the art of witchcraft from her mother, she sewed a charm inside them. And once when the King had ridden forth to hunt, she took the little shirts and went into the forest, and the ball showed her the way.

The children, who saw from a distance that someone was approaching, thought that their dear father was coming to them, and full of joy, ran to meet him. Then she threw one of the little shirts over each of them, and no sooner had the shirts touched their bodies than they were changed into swans, and flew away over the forest. The Queen went home quite delighted, and thought she had got rid of her step-children, but the girl had not run out with her brothers, and the Queen knew nothing about her. Next day, the King went to visit his children, but he found no one but the little girl.

'Where are thy brothers?' asked the King.

'Alas, dear father,' she answered, 'they have gone away and left me alone!' And she told him that she had seen from her little window how her brothers had flown away over the forest in the shape of swans, and she showed him the feathers, which they had let fall in the courtyard, and which she had picked up. The King mourned, but he did not think that the Queen had done this wicked deed, and as he feared that the girl would also be stolen away from him, he wanted to take her away with him. But she was afraid of her step-mother, and entreated the King to let her stay just this one night more in the forest castle.

The poor girl thought, 'I can no longer stay here. I will go and seek my brothers.' And when night came, she ran away, and went straight into the forest. She walked the whole night long, and next day also without stopping, until she could go no farther for weariness. Then she saw a forest hut, and went into it, and found a room with six little beds, but she did not venture to get into one of them, but crept under one, and lay down on the hard ground, intending to pass the night there. Just before sunset, however, she heard a rustling, and saw six swans come flying in at the window. They alighted on the ground and blew at each other, and blew all the feathers off, and their swans' skins stripped off like a shirt. Then the maiden looked at them and recognized her brothers, was glad and crept forth from beneath the bed. The brothers were no less delighted to see their little sister, but their joy was of short duration.

'Here canst thou not abide,' they said to her. 'This is a shelter for robbers. If they come home and find thee, they will kill thee.'

'But can you not protect me?' asked the little sister.

'No,' they replied, 'only for one quarter of an hour each evening can we lay aside our swans' skins and have during that time our human form; after that, we are once more turned into swans.'

The little sister wept and said, 'Can you not be set free?'

'Alas, no,' they answered, 'the conditions are too hard! For six years thou mayst neither speak nor laugh, and in that time thou must sew together six little shirts of starwort for us. And if one single word falls from thy lips, all thy work will be lost.' And when the brothers had said this, the quarter of an hour was over, and they flew out of the window again as swans.

The maiden, however, firmly resolved to deliver her brothers, even if it should cost her her life. She left the hut, went into the midst of the forest, seated herself on a tree, and there passed the night. Next morning she went out and gathered starwort and began to sew. She could not speak to any one, and she had no inclination to laugh; she sat there and looked at nothing but her work.

When she had already spent a long time there. it came to pass that the King of the country was hunting in the forest, and his huntsmen came to the tree on which the maiden was sitting. They called to her and said, 'Who art thou?' But she made no answer. 'Come down to us,' said they. 'We will not do thee any harm.' She only shook her head.

As they pressed her further with questions she threw her golden necklace down to them, and thought to content them thus. They, however, did not cease, and then she threw her girdle down to them, and as this also was to no purpose, her garters, and by degrees everything that she had on that she could do without until she had nothing left but her shift. The huntsmen, however, did not let themselves be turned aside by that, but climbed the tree and fetched the maiden down and led her before the King.

The King asked, 'Who art thou? What art thou doing on the

tree?' But she did not answer. He put the question in every language that he knew, but she remained as mute as a fish. As she was so beautiful, the King's heart was touched, and he was smitten with a great love for her. He put his mantle on her, took her before him on his horse, and carried her to his castle. Then he caused her to be dressed in rich garments, and she shone in her beauty like bright daylight, but no word could be drawn from her. He placed her by his side at table, and her modest bearing and courtesy pleased him so much that he said, 'She is the one whom I wish to marry, and no other woman in the world.' And after some days he united himself to her.

The King, however, had a wicked mother who was dissatisfied with this marriage and spoke ill of the young Queen. 'Who knows,' said she, 'from whence the creature who can't speak, comes? She is not worthy of a king!'

After a year had passed, when the Queen brought her first child into the world, the old woman took it away from her, and smeared her mouth with blood as she slept. Then she went to the King and accused the Queen of being a man-eater. The King would not believe it, and would not suffer anyone to do her any injury. She, however, sat continually sewing at the shirts, and cared for nothing else. The next time, when she again bore a beautiful boy, the false step-mother used the same treachery, but the King could not bring himself to give credit to her words. He said, 'She is too pious and good to do anything of that kind; if she were not dumb, and could defend herself, her innocence would come to light.'

But when the old woman stole away the newly born child for the third time, and accused the Queen, who did not utter one word of defence, the King could do no otherwise than deliver her over to justice, and she was sentenced to suffer death by fire.

When the day came for the sentence to be executed, it was the last day of the six years during which she was not to speak or laugh, and she had delivered her dear brothers from the power of the enchantment. The six shirts were ready, only the left sleeve of the sixth was wanting. When, therefore, she was led to the stake, she laid the shirts on her arm, and when she stood on high and the fire was just going to be lighted, she looked around and six swans came flying through the air towards her. Then she saw that her deliverance was near, and her heart leapt with joy. The swans swept towards her and sank down so that she could throw the shirts over them, and as they were touched by them, their swans' skins fell off, and her brothers stood in their own bodily form before her, and were vigorous and handsome. The youngest only lacked his left arm, and had in the place of it a swan's wing on his shoulder. They embraced and kissed each other, and the Queen went to the King, who was greatly moved, and she began to speak and said, 'Dearest husband, now I may speak and declare to thee that I am innocent, and falsely accused.' And she told him of the treachery of the old woman who had taken away her three children and hidden them. Then to the great joy of the King they were brought thither, and as a punishment, the wicked step-mother was bound to the stake, and burnt to ashes. But the King and the Queen with their six brothers lived many years in happiness and peace.

BRIAR-ROSE

A long time ago, there were a King and Queen who said every day, 'Ah, if only we had a child!' but they never had one. But it happened that once when the Queen was bathing, a frog crept out of the water on to the land, and said to her, 'Your wish shall be fulfilled; before a year has gone by, you shall have a daughter.'

What the frog had said came true, and the Queen had a little girl who was so pretty that the King could not contain himself for joy, and ordered a great feast. He invited not only his kindred, friends and acquaintance, but also the Wise Women, in order that they might be kind and well-disposed towards the child. There were thirteen of them in his kingdom, but, as he had only twelve golden plates for them to eat out of, one of them had to be left at home.

The feast was held with all manner of splendour and when it came to an end the Wise Women bestowed their magic gifts upon the baby: one gave virtue, another beauty, a third riches, and so on with everything in the world that one can wish for.

When eleven of them had made their promises, suddenly the thirteenth came in. She wished to avenge herself for not having been invited, and without greeting, or even looking at any one, she cried with a loud voice, 'The King's daughter shall in her fifteenth year prick herself with a spindle, and fall down dead.' And, without saying a word more, she turned round and left the room.

They were all shocked; but the twelfth, whose good wish still remained unspoken, came forward, and as she could not undo the evil sentence, but only soften it, she said, 'It shall not be death, but a deep sleep of a hundred years, into which the princess shall fall.'

The King, who would fain keep his dear child from the misfortune, gave orders that every spindle in the whole kingdom should be burnt. Meanwhile, the gifts of the Wise Women were plenteously fulfilled on the young girl, for she was so beautiful, modest, good-natured and wise, that everyone who saw her was bound to love her.

It happened that on the very day when she was fifteen years old, the King and Queen were not at home, and the maiden was left in the palace quite alone. So she went round into all sorts of places, looked into rooms and bed-chambers just as she liked, and at last came to an old tower. She climbed up the narrow, winding staircase, and reached a little door. A rusty key was in the lock, and when she turned it the door sprang open, and there in a little room sat an old woman with a spindle, busily spinning her flax.

'Good day, old dame,' said the King's daughter; 'what are you doing there?'

'I am spinning,' said the old woman, and nodded her head. 'What sort of thing is that, that rattles round so merrily?' said the girl, and she took the spindle and wanted to spin too. But scarcely had she touched the spindle when the magic decree was fulfilled, and she pricked her finger with it.

And, in the very moment when she felt the prick, she fell down upon the bed that stood there, and lay in a deep sleep. And this sleep extended over the whole palace; the King and Queen who had just come home, and had entered the great hall, began to go to sleep, and the whole of the court with them. The horses, too, went to sleep in the stable, the dogs in the yard, the pigeons upon the roof, the flies on the wall; even the fire that was flaming on the hearth became quiet and slept, the roast meat left off frizzling, and the cook, who was just going to pull the hair of the scullery boy, because he had forgotten something, let him go, and went to sleep. And the wind fell, and on the trees before the castle not a leaf moved again.

But round about the castle there began to grow a hedge of thorns, which every year became higher, and at last grew close up round the castle and all over it, so that there was nothing of it to be seen, not even the flag upon the roof. But the story of the beautiful sleeping 'Briar-Rose', for so the princess was named, went about the country, so that from time to time kings' sons came and tried to get through the thorny hedge into the castle.

But they found it impossible, for the thorns held fast together, as if they had hands, and the youths were caught in them, could not get loose again, and died a miserable death.

After long, long years a King's son came again to that country, and heard an old man talking about the thorn-hedge, and that a castle was said to stand behind it in which a wonderfully beautiful princess, named Briar-rose, had been asleep for a hundred years; and that the King and Queen and the whole court were asleep likewise. He had heard, too, from his grandfather, that many kings' sons had already come, and had tried to get through the thorny hedge, but they had remained sticking fast in it, and had died a pitiful death. Then the youth said, 'I am not afraid, I will go and see the beautiful Briar-Rose.' The good old man might dissuade him as he would, he did not listen to his words.

But by this time the hundred years had just passed, and the

day had come when Briar-Rose was to awake again. When the King's son came near to the thorn-hedge, it was nothing but large and beautiful flowers, which parted from each other of their own accord, and let him pass unhurt, then they closed again behind him like a hedge. In the castle yard, he saw the horses and the spotted hounds lying asleep; on the roof sat the pigeons with their heads under their wings. And when he entered the house, the flies were asleep upon the wall, the cook in the kitchen was still holding out his hand to seize the boy, and the maid was sitting by the black hen which she was going to pluck.

He went on farther, and in the great hall he saw the whole of the court lying asleep, and up by the throne lay the King and Queen.

Then he went on still farther, and all was so quiet that a breath could be heard, and at last he came to the tower, and opened the door into the little room where Briar-Rose was sleeping. There she lay, so beautiful that he could not turn his eyes away; and he stooped down and gave her a kiss. But as soon as he kissed her, Briar-Rose opened her eyes and awoke, and looked at him quite sweetly.

Then they went down together, and the King awoke, and the Queen, and the whole court, and looked at each other in great astonishment. And the horses in the courtyard stood up and shook themselves; the hounds jumped up and wagged their tails; the pigeons upon the roof pulled out their heads from under their wings, looked round, and flew into the open country; the flies on the wall crept again; the fire in the kitchen burned up and flickered and cooked the meat; the joint began to turn and frizzle again, and the cook gave the boy such a box on the ear that he screamed, and the maid plucked the fowl ready for the spit.

And then the marriage of the King's son with Briar-Rose was celebrated with all splendour, and they lived contented to the end of their days.

LITTLE SNOW-WHITE

Once upon a time in the middle of winter, when the flakes of snow were falling like feathers from the sky, a queen sat at a window sewing, and the frame of the window was made of black ebony. And whilst she was sewing and looking out of the window at the snow, she pricked her finger with the needle, and three drops of blood fell upon the snow. And the red looked pretty upon the white snow, and she thought to herself, 'Would that I had a child as white as snow, as red as blood, and as black as the wood of the window-frame.'

Soon after that she had a little daughter, who was as white as snow, and as red as blood, and her hair was as black as ebony; and she was therefore called Little Snow-White. And when the child was born, the Queen died.

After a year had passed the King took to himself another wife. She was a beautiful woman, but proud and haughty, and she could not bear that anyone else should surpass her in beauty. She had a wonderful looking-glass, and when she stood in front of it and looked at herself in it, and said,

'Looking-glass, Looking-glass, on the wall,
Who in this land is the fairest of all?',

the looking-glass answered:

'Thou, O Queen, art the fairest of all!'

Then she was satisfied, for she knew that the looking-glass spoke the truth.

But Snow-White was growing up, and grew more and more beautiful; and when she was seven years old she was as beautiful as the day, and more beautiful than the Queen herself. And once when the Queen asked her looking-glass,

'Looking-glass, Looking-glass, on the wall,
Who in this land is the fairest of all?'

it answered,

'Thou art fairer than all who are here, Lady Queen.
But more beautiful still is Snow-White, as I ween.'

Then the Queen was shocked, and turned yellow and green with envy. From that hour, whenever she looked at Snow-White, her heart heaved in her breast, she hated the girl so much.

And envy and pride grew higher and higher in her heart like a weed, so that she had no peace day or night. She called a huntsman, and said, 'Take the child away into the forest; I will no longer have her in my sight. Kill her, and bring me back her heart as a token.' The huntsman obeyed, and took her away; but when he had drawn his knife, and was about to pierce Snow-White's innocent heart, she began to weep, and said, 'Ah dear huntsman, leave me my life! I will run away into the wild forest, and never come home again.'

And as she was so beautiful the huntsman had pity on her and said, 'Run away, then, you poor child.' 'The wild beasts will soon have devoured you,' thought he, and yet it seemed as if a stone had been rolled from his heart since it was no longer needful for him to kill her. And as a young boar just then came running by he stabbed it, and cut out its heart and took it to the Queen as proof that the child was dead. The cook had to salt this, and the wicked Queen ate it, and thought she had eaten the heart of Snow-White.

But now the poor child was all alone in the great forest, and so terrified that she looked at every leaf of every tree, and did not know what to do. Then she began to run, and ran over sharp stones and through thorns, and the wild beasts ran past her, but did her no harm.

She ran as long as her feet would go until it was almost evening; then she saw a little cottage and went into it to rest herself. Everything in the cottage was small, but neater and cleaner than can be told. There was a table on which was a white cover, and seven little plates, and on each plate a little spoon; moreover, there were seven little knives and forks, and seven little mugs. Against the wall stood seven little beds side by side, and covered with snow-white counterpanes.

Little Snow-White was so hungry and thirsty that she ate some vegetables and bread from each plate and drank a drop of wine out of each mug, for she did not wish to take all from one only. Then, as she was so tired, she laid herself down on one of the little beds, but none of them suited her; one was too long, another too short, but at last she found that the seventh one was right, and so she remained in it, said a prayer and went to sleep.

When it was quite dark the owners of the cottage came back; they were seven dwarfs who dug and delved in the mountains for ore. They lit their seven candles, and as it was now light within the cottage they saw that someone had been there, for everything was not in the same order in which they had left it.

The first said, 'Who has been sitting on my chair?'

The second, 'Who has been eating off my plate?'

The third, 'Who has been taking some of my bread?'

The fourth, 'Who has been eating my vegetables?'

The fifth, 'Who has been using my fork?'

The sixth, 'Who has been cutting with my knife?'

The seventh, 'Who has been drinking out of my mug?'

Then the first looked round and saw that there was a little hole on his bed, and he said, 'Who has been getting into my bed?' The others came up and each called out, 'Somebody has been lying in my bed too.' But the seventh when he looked at his bed saw little Snow-White, who was lying asleep therein. And he called the others, who came running up, and they cried out with astonishment, and brought their seven little candles and let the light fall on little Snow-White. 'Oh, heavens! oh, heavens!' cried they, 'what a lovely child!' and they were so glad that they did not wake her up, but let her sleep on in the bed. And the seventh dwarf slept with his companions, one hour with each, and so got through the night.

When it was morning little Snow-White awoke, and was frightened when she saw the seven dwarfs. But they were friendly and asked her what her name was. 'My name is Snow-White,' she answered. 'How have you come to our house?' said the dwarfs. Then she told them that her step-mother had wished to have her killed, but that the huntsman had spared her life, and that she had run for the whole day, until at last she had found their dwelling. The dwarfs said, 'If you will take care of our house, cook, make the beds, wash, sew, and knit, and if you will keep everything neat and clean, you can stay with us and you shall want for nothing.'

'Yes,' said Snow-White, 'with all my heart,' and she stayed with them. She kept the house in order for them; in the mornings they went to the mountains and looked for copper and gold, in the evenings they came back, and then their supper had to be ready. The girl was alone the whole day, so the good dwarfs warned her and said, 'Beware of your step-mother, she will soon know that you are here; be sure to let no one come in.'

But the Queen, believing that she had eaten Snow-White's heart, could not but think that she was again the first and most beautiful of all; and she went to her looking-glass and said,

'Looking-glass, Looking-glass, on the wall,
Who in this land is the fairest of all?'

and the glass answered:

'Oh, Queen, thou art fairest of all I see,
But over the hills, where the seven dwarfs dwell,
Snow-White is still alive and well,
And none is so fair as she.'

Then she was astounded, for she knew that the looking-glass never spoke falsely, and she knew that the huntsman had betrayed her, and that little Snow-White was still alive.

And so she thought and thought again how she might kill her, for so long as she was not the fairest in the whole land, envy let her have no rest. And when she had at last thought of something to do, she painted her face, and dressed herself like an old pedlar-woman, and no one could have known her. In this disguise she went over the seven mountains to the seven dwarfs, and knocked at the door and cried, 'Pretty things to sell, very cheap, very cheap.' Little Snow-White looked out of the window and called out, 'Good-day my good woman, what have you to sell?'

'Good things, pretty things,' she answered; 'stay-laces of all colours,' and she pulled out one which was woven of bright-coloured silk. 'I may let the worthy old woman in,' thought Snow-White, and she unbolted the door and bought the pretty laces. 'Child,' said the old woman, 'what a fright you look; come, I will lace you properly for once.'

Snow-White had no suspicion, but stood before her, and let herself be laced with the new laces. But the old woman laced so quickly and so tightly that Snow-White lost her breath and fell down as if dead. 'Now I am the most beautiful,' said the Queen to herself, and ran away.

Not long afterwards, in the evening, the seven dwarfs came home, but how shocked they were when they saw their dear little Snow-White lying on the ground, and that she neither stirred nor moved, and seemed to be dead. They lifted her up, and, as they saw that she was laced too tightly, they cut the laces; then she began to breathe a little, and after a while came to life again. When the dwarfs heard what had happened they said, 'The old pedlar-woman was no one else than the wicked Queen; take care and let no one come in when we are not with you.'

But the wicked woman when she had reached home went in front of the glass and asked,

'Looking-glass, Looking-glass, on the wall,
Who in this land is the fairest of all?'

and it answered as before:

> 'Oh, Queen, thou art fairest of all I see,
> But over the hills, where the seven dwarfs dwell,
> Snow-White is still alive and well,
> And none is so fair as she.'

When she heard that, all her blood rushed to her heart with fear, for she saw plainly that little Snow-White was again alive. 'But now,' she said, 'I will think of something that shall put an end to you,' and by the help of witchcraft, which she understood, she made a poisonous comb. Then she disguised herself and took the shape of another old woman. So she went over the seven mountains to the seven dwarfs, knocked at the door, and cried, 'Good things to sell, cheap, cheap!'

Little Snow-White looked out and said, 'Go away; I cannot let anyone come in.'

'I suppose you can look,' said the old woman, and pulled the poisonous comb out and held it up. It pleased the girl so well that she let herself be beguiled, and opened the door. When they had made a bargain the old woman said, 'Now I will comb you properly for once.' Poor little Snow-White had no suspicion, and let the old woman do as she pleased, but hardly had she put the comb in her hair than the poison in it took effect, and the girl fell down senseless. 'You paragon of beauty,' said the wicked woman, 'you are done for now,' and she went away.

But fortunately it was almost evening, when the seven dwarfs came home. When they saw Snow-White lying as if dead upon the ground they at once suspected the step-mother, and they looked and found the poisoned comb. Scarcely had they taken it out when Snow-White came to herself, and told them what had happened.

Then they warned her once more to be upon her guard and to open the door to no one.

The Queen, at home, went in front of the glass and said,

'Looking-glass, Looking-glass, on the wall,
Who in this land is the fairest of all?'

then it answered as before:

'Oh, Queen, thou art fairest of all I see,
But over the hills, where the seven dwarfs dwell,
Snow-White is still alive and well,
And none is so fair as she.'

When she heard the glass speak thus she trembled and shook with rage. 'Snow-White shall die,' she cried, 'even if it costs me my life!'

Thereupon she went into a quite secret, lonely room, where no one ever came, and there she made a very poisonous apple. Outside it looked pretty, white with a red cheek, so that everyone who saw it longed for it; but whoever ate a piece of it must surely die.

When the apple was ready she painted her face, and dressed herself up as a country woman, and so she went over the seven mountains to the seven dwarfs. She knocked at the door. Snow-White put her head out of the window and said, 'I cannot let any one in; the seven dwarfs have forbidden me.'

'It is all the same to me,' answered the woman, 'I shall soon get rid of my apples. There, I will give you one.'

'No,' said Snow-White, 'I dare not take anything.'

'Are you afraid of poison?' said the old woman; 'look, I will cut the apple in two pieces; you eat the red cheek, and I will eat the white.' The apple was so cunningly made that only the red cheek was poisoned. Snow-White longed for the fine apple, and when she saw that the woman ate part of it she could resist no longer, and stretched out her hand and took the poisonous half. But hardly had she a bit of it in her mouth than she fell down dead. Then the Queen looked at her with a dreadful look, and laughed aloud and said, 'White as snow, red as blood, black as ebony-wood! this time the dwarfs cannot wake you up again.'

And when she asked of the Looking-glass at home,

'Looking-glass, Looking-glass, on the wall,
Who in this land is the fairest of all?'

it answered at last:

'Oh, Queen, in this land thou art fairest of all.'

Then her envious heart had rest, so far as an envious heart can have rest.

The dwarfs, when they came home in the evening, found Snow-White lying upon the ground; she breathed no longer and was dead. They lifted her up, looked to see whether they could find anything poisonous, unlaced her, combed her hair, washed her with water and wine, but it was all of no use; the poor child was dead, and remained dead. They laid her upon a bier, and all seven of them sat round it and wept for her, and wept three days long.

Then they were going to bury her, but she still looked as if she were living, and still had her pretty red cheeks. They said,

'We could not bury her in the dark ground,' and they had a transparent coffin of glass made, so that she could be seen from all sides, and they laid her in it, and wrote her name upon it in golden letters, and that she was a king's daughter. Then they put the coffin out upon the mountain, and one of them always stayed by it and watched it. And birds came too, and wept for Snow-White; first an owl, then a raven, and last a dove.

And now Snow-White lay a long, long time in the coffin, and she did not change, but looked as if she were asleep; for she was as white as snow, as red as blood, and her hair was as black as ebony.

It happened, however, that a king's son came into the forest, and went to the dwarves' house to spend the night. He saw the coffin on the mountain, and the beautiful Snow-White within it, and read what was written upon it in golden letters. Then he said to the dwarfs, 'Let me have the coffin, I will give you whatever you want for it.' But the dwarfs answered, 'We will not part with it for all the gold in the world.' Then he said, 'Let me have it as a gift, for I cannot live without seeing Snow-White. I will honour and prize her as my dearest possession.' As he spoke in this way the good dwarfs took pity upon him, and gave him the coffin.

And now the King's son had it carried away by his servants on their shoulders. And it happened that they stumbled over a tree-stump, and with the shock the poisonous piece of apple which Snow-White had bitten off came out of her throat. And before long she opened her eyes, lifted up the lid of the coffin, sat up, and was once more alive. 'Oh, heavens, where am I?' she cried. The King's son, full of joy, said, 'You are with me,' and told her what had happened, and said, 'I love you more than everything in the world; come with me to my father's palace, you shall be my wife.'

And Snow-White was willing, and went with him, and their wedding was held with great show and splendour. But Snow-White's wicked step-mother was also bidden to the feast. When she had arrayed herself in beautiful clothes she went before the Looking-glass, and said,

'Looking-glass, Looking-glass, on the wall,
Who in this land is the fairest of all?'

the glass answered,

'Oh, Queen, of all here the fairest art thou,
But the young Queen is fairer by far as I trow.'

Then the wicked woman uttered a curse, and was so wretched, so utterly wretched, that she knew not what to do. At first she would not go to the wedding at all, but she had no peace, and must go to see the young Queen. And when she went in she knew Snow-White; and she stood still with rage and fear, and could not stir. But iron slippers had already been put upon the fire, and they were brought in with tongs, and set before her. Then she was forced to put on the red-hot shoes, and dance until she dropped down dead.

RUMPELSTILTSKIN

Once there was a miller who was poor, but who had a beautiful daughter. Now it happened that he had to go and speak to the King, and in order to make himself appear important he said to him, 'I have a daughter who can spin straw into gold.' The King said to the miller, 'That is an art which pleases me well; if your daughter is as clever as you say, bring her tomorrow to my palace, and I will try what she can do.'

And when the girl was brought to him he took her into a room which was quite full of straw, gave her a spinning-wheel and a reel, and said, 'Now set to work, and if by tomorrow morning early you have not spun this straw into gold during the night, you must die.' Thereupon he himself locked up the room, and left her in it alone. So there sat the poor miller's daughter, and for the life of her could not decide what to do; she had no idea how straw could be spun into gold, and she grew more and more miserable, until at last she began to weep.

But all at once the door opened, and in came a little man, and said, 'Good evening, Mistress Miller; why are you crying so?'

'Alas!' answered the girl, 'I have to spin straw into gold, and I do not know how to do it.'

'What will you give me,' said the manikin, 'if I do it for you?'

'My necklace,' said the girl.

The little man took the necklace, seated himself in front of the wheel, and 'whirr, whirr, whirr,' three turns, and the reel was full; then he put another on, and 'whirr, whirr, whirr,' three times round, and the second was full too. And so it went on until the morning, when all the straw was spun, and all the reels were full of gold. By daybreak the King was already there, and when he saw the gold he was astonished and delighted, but his heart became only more greedy. He had the miller's daughter taken into another room full of straw, which was much larger, and commanded her to spin that also in one night if she valued her life. The girl knew not how to help herself, and was crying, when the door again opened, and the little man appeared, and said, 'What will you give me if I spin that straw into gold for you?'

'The ring on my finger,' answered the girl. The little man took the ring, again began to turn the wheel, and by morning had spun all the straw into glittering gold.

The King rejoiced beyond measure at the sight, but still he had not gold enough; and he had the miller's daughter taken into a still larger room full of straw, and said, 'You must spin this, too, in the course of this night; but if you succeed, you shall be my wife.'

'Even if she be a miller's daughter,' thought he, 'I could not find a richer wife in the whole world.'

When the girl was alone the manikin came again for the third time, and said, 'What will you give me if I spin the straw for you this time also?'

'I have nothing left that I could give,' answered the girl.

'Then promise me, if you should become Queen, your first child.'

'Who knows whether that will ever happen?' thought the miller's daughter; and, not knowing how else to help herself in this strait, she promised the manikin what he wanted, and for that he once more span the straw into gold.

And when the King came in the morning, and found all as he had wished, he took her in marriage, and the pretty miller's daughter became a Queen.

A year after, she had a beautiful child, and she never gave a thought to the manikin. But suddenly he came into her room, and said, 'Now give me what you promised.' The Queen was horror-struck, and offered the manikin all the riches of the kingdom if he would leave her the child. But the manikin said, 'No, something that is living is dearer to me than all the treasures in the world.' Then the Queen began to weep and cry, so that the manikin pitied her. 'I will give you three days' time,' said he, 'if by that time you find out my name, then shall you keep your child.'

So the Queen thought the whole night of all the names that she had ever heard, and she sent a messenger over the country to enquire, far and wide, for any other names that there might be. When the manikin came the next day, she began with Caspar, Melchior, Balthazar, and said all the names she knew, one after another; but to every one the little man said, 'That is not my name.' On the second day, she had enquiries made in the neighbourhood as to the names of the people there, and she repeated to the manikin the most uncommon and curious. 'Perhaps your name is Shortribs, or Sheepshanks, or Laceleg?' but he always answered, 'That is not my name.'

On the third day, the messenger came back again, and said, 'I have not been able to find a single new name, but as I came to a high mountain at the end of the forest, where the fox and the hare bid each other good night, there I saw a little house, and before the house a fire was burning, and round about the fire quite a ridiculous little man was jumping: he hopped upon one leg, and shouted,

'Today I bake, tomorrow brew,
The next I'll have the young Queen's child.
Ha! glad am I that no one knew
That Rumpelstiltskin I am styled.'

You may think how glad the Queen was when she heard the name! And when soon afterwards the little man came in, and asked, 'Now, Mistress Queen, what is my name?' at first she said, 'Is your name Conrad?'

'No.'

'Is your name Harry?'

'No.'

'Perhaps your name is Rumpelstiltskin?'

'The devil has told you that! the devil has told you that!' cried the little man, and in his anger he plunged his right foot so deep into the earth that his whole leg went in; and then in rage he pulled at his left leg so hard with both hands that he tore himself in two.

THE GOLDEN GOOSE

There was a man who had three sons, the youngest of whom was called Dummling[1], and was despised, mocked, and put down on every occasion.

It happened that the eldest wanted to go into the forest to hew wood, and before he went his mother gave him a beautiful sweet cake and a bottle of wine in order that he might not suffer from hunger or thirst.

When he entered the forest there met him a little grey-haired old man who bade him good-day, and said, 'Do give me a piece of cake out of your pocket, and let me have a draught of your wine; I am so hungry and thirsty.' But the prudent youth answered, 'If I give you my cake and wine, I shall have none for myself; be off with you,' and he left the little man standing and went on.

But when he began to hew down a tree, it was not long before he made a false stroke, and the axe cut him in the arm, so that he had to go home and have it bound up. And this was the little grey man's doing.

After this the second son went into the forest, and his mother gave him, like the eldest, a cake and a bottle of wine. The little old grey man met him likewise, and asked him for a piece of cake and a drink of wine. But the second son, too, said with much reason, 'What I give you will be taken away from myself; be off!' and he left the little man standing and went on. His punishment, however, was not delayed; when he had made a few

---

[1] Simpleton.

THE GOLDEN GOOSE

strokes at the tree he struck himself in the leg, so that he had to be carried home.

Then Dummling said, 'Father, do let me go and cut wood.' The father answered, 'Your brothers have hurt themselves with it, leave it alone, you do not understand anything about it.' But Dummling begged so long that at last he said, 'Just go then, you will get wiser by hurting yourself.' His mother gave him a cake made with water and baked in the cinders, and with it a bottle of sour beer.

When he came to the forest the little old grey man met him likewise, and greeting him, said, 'Give me a piece of your cake and a drink out of your bottle; I am so hungry and thirsty.' Dummling answered, 'I have only cinder-cake and sour beer; if that pleases you, we will sit down and eat.' So they sat down, and when Dummling pulled out his cinder-cake, it was a fine sweet cake, and the sour beer had become good wine. So they ate and drank, and after that the little man said, 'Since you have a good heart, and are willing to divide what you have, I will give you good luck. There stands an old tree, cut it down, and you will find something at the roots.' Then the little man took leave of him.

Dummling went and cut down the tree, and when it fell there was a goose sitting in the roots with feathers of pure gold. He lifted her up, and taking her with him, went to an inn where he thought he would stay the night. Now the host had three daughters, who saw the goose and were curious to know what such a wonderful bird might be, and would have liked to have one of its golden feathers.

The eldest thought, 'I shall soon find an opportunity of pulling out a feather,' and as soon as Dummling had gone out she seized the goose by the wing, but her finger and hand remained sticking fast to it.

The second came soon afterwards, thinking only of how she might get a feather for herself, but she had scarcely touched her sister than she was held fast.

At last the third also came with the like intent, and the others screamed out, 'Keep away; for goodness' sake keep away!' But she did not understand why she was to keep away. 'The others are there,' she thought, 'I may as well be there too,' and ran to them; but as soon as she had touched her sister, she remained sticking fast to her. So they had to spend the night with the goose.

The next morning Dummling took the goose under his arm and set out, without troubling himself about the three girls who were hanging on to it. They were obliged to run after him continually, now left, now right, just as he was inclined to go.

In the middle of the fields the parson met them, and when he saw the procession he said, "For shame, you good-for-nothing girls, why are you running across the fields after this young man? Is that seemly?" At the same time he seized the youngest by the hand in order to pull her away, but as soon as he touched her he likewise stuck fast, and was himself obliged to run behind.

Before long the sexton came by and saw his master, the parson, running behind three girls. He was astonished at this and called out, 'Hi, your reverence, whither away so quickly? Do not forget that we have a christening today!' and running after him he took him by the sleeve, but was also held fast to it.

Whilst the five were trotting thus one behind the other, two labourers came with their hoes from the fields; the parson called out to them and begged that they would set him and the sexton free. But they had scarcely touched the sexton when they were held fast, and now there were seven of them running behind Dummling and the goose.

Soon afterwards he came to a city, where a king ruled who had a daughter who was so serious that no one could make her laugh. So he had put forth a decree that whosoever should be able to make her laugh should marry her. When Dummling heard this, he went with his goose and all her train before the King's daughter, and as soon as she saw the seven people running on and on, one behind the other, she began to laugh quite loudly, and as if she would never leave off. Thereupon Dummling asked to have her for his wife, and the wedding was celebrated. After the King's death, Dummling inherited the kingdom and lived a long time contentedly with his wife.

JORINDA AND JORINGEL[1]

There was once an old castle in the midst of a large and thick forest, and in it an old woman who was a witch dwelt all alone. In the daytime she changed herself into a cat or a screech-owl, but in the evening she took her proper shape again as a human being. She could lure wild beasts and birds to her, and then she killed and boiled and roasted them. If anyone came within one hundred paces of the castle he was obliged to stand still, and could not stir from the place until she bade him be free. But whenever an innocent maiden came within this circle, she changed her into a bird, and shut her up in a wicker-work cage, and carried the cage into a room in the castle. She had about seven thousand cages of rare birds in the castle.

Now, there was once a maiden who was called Jorinda, who was fairer than all other girls. She and a handsome youth named Joringel had promised to marry each other. They were still in the days of betrothal, and their greatest happiness was being together. One day in order that they might be able to talk together in quiet they went for a walk in the forest. 'Take care,' said Joringel, 'that you do not go too near the castle.'

It was a beautiful evening; the sun shone brightly between the trunks of the trees into the dark green of the forest, and the turtle-doves sang mournfully upon the young boughs of the birch-trees.

Jorinda wept now and then: she sat down in the sunshine and was sorrowful. Joringel was sorrowful too; they were as sad as

---

[1] Jorinker, a bird of the titmouse species. It is said to be named from its cry.

if they were about to die. Then they looked around them, and were quite at a loss, for they did not know by which way they should go home. The sun was still half above the mountain and half set.

Joringel looked through the bushes, and saw the old walls of the castle close at hand. He was horror-stricken and filled with deadly fear. Jorinda was singing:

> 'My little bird, with the necklace red,
> Sings sorrow, sorrow, sorrow,
> He sings that the dove must soon be dead,
> Sings sorrow, sor – jug, jug, jug.'

Joringel looked for Jorinda. She was changed into a nightingale, and sang, 'Jug, jug, jug.' A screech-owl with glowing eyes flew three times round about her, and three times cried, 'to-whoo, to-whoo, to-whoo!'

Joringel could not move: he stood there like a stone, and could neither weep nor speak, nor move hand or foot.

The sun had now set. The owl flew into the thicket, and directly afterwards there came out of it a crooked old woman, yellow and lean, with large red eyes and a hooked nose, the point of which reached to her chin. She muttered to herself, caught the nightingale, and took it away in her hand.

Joringel could neither speak nor move from the spot; the nightingale was gone. At last the woman came back, and said in a hollow voice, 'Greet thee, Zachiel. If the moon shines on the cage, Zachiel, let him loose at once.' Then Joringel was freed. He fell on his knees before the woman and begged that she would give him back his Jorinda, but she said that he should never have her again, and went away. He called, he wept, he lamented, but all in vain, 'Ah, what is to become of me?'

Joringel went away, and at last came to a strange village; there he kept sheep for a long time. He often walked round and round the castle, but not too near to it. At last he dreamt one night that he found a blood-red flower, in the middle of which was a beautiful large pearl; that he picked the flower and went with it to the castle, and that everything he touched with the flower was freed from enchantment; he also dreamt that by means of it he recovered his Jorinda.

In the morning, when he awoke, he began to seek over hill and dale if he could find such a flower. He sought until the ninth day, and then, early in the morning, he found the blood-red flower. In the middle of it there was a large dew-drop, as big as the finest pearl.

Day and night he journeyed with this flower to the castle. When he was within a hundred paces of it he was not held fast, but walked on to the door. Joringel was full of joy; he touched the door with the flower, and it sprang open. He walked in through the courtyard, and listened for the sound of the birds. At last he heard it. He went on and found the room from whence it came, and there the witch was feeding the birds in the seven thousand cages.

When she saw Joringel she was angry, very angry, and scolded and spat poison and gall at him, but she could not come within two paces of him. He did not take any notice of her, but went and looked at the cages with the birds; but there were many hundred nightingales, how was he to find his Jorinda again?

Just then he saw the old woman quietly take away a cage with a bird in it, and go towards the door.

Swiftly he sprang towards her, touched the cage with the flower, and also the old woman. She could now no longer bewitch anyone; and Jorinda was standing there, clasping him round the neck, and she was as beautiful as ever!

THE OLD MAN AND HIS GRANDSON

There was once a very old man, whose eyes had become dim, his ears dull of hearing, his knees trembled, and when he sat at table he could hardly hold the spoon, and spilt the broth upon the tablecloth or let it run out of his mouth. His son and his son's wife were disgusted at this, so the old grandfather at last had to sit in the corner behind the stove, and they gave him his food in an earthenware bowl, and not even enough of it. And he used to look towards the table with his eyes full of tears. Once, too, his trembling hands could not hold the bowl, and it fell to the ground and broke. The young wife scolded him, but he said nothing and only sighed. Then they bought him a wooden bowl for a few halfpence, out of which he had to eat.

They were once sitting thus when the little grandson of four years old began to gather together some bits of wood upon the ground. 'What are you doing there?' asked the father.

'I am making a little trough,' answered the child, 'for father and mother to eat out of when I am big.'

The man and his wife looked at each other for a while, and presently began to cry. Then they took the old grandfather to the table, and henceforth always let him eat with them, and likewise said nothing if he did spill a little of anything.

THE GOOSE-GIRL

There was once upon a time an old Queen whose husband had been dead for many years, and she had a beautiful daughter. When the princess grew up she was betrothed to a prince who lived at a great distance. When the time came for her to be married, and she had to journey forth into the distant kingdom, the aged Queen packed up for her many costly vessels of silver and gold, and trinkets also of gold and silver; and cups and jewels, in short, everything which appertained to a royal dowry, for she loved her child with all her heart. She likewise sent her maid in waiting, who was to ride with her, and hand her over to the bridegroom, and each had a horse for the journey, but the horse of the King's daughter was called Falada, and could speak. So when the hour of parting had come, the aged mother went into her bedroom, took a small knife and cut her finger with it until it bled, then she held a white handkerchief to it into which she let three drops of blood fall, gave it to her daughter and said, 'Dear child, preserve this carefully, it will be of service to you on your way.'

So they took a sorrowful leave of each other; the princess put the piece of cloth in her bosom, mounted her horse, and then went away to her bridegroom. After she had ridden for a while she felt a burning thirst, and said to her waiting-maid, 'Dismount, and take my cup which thou hast brought with thee for me, and get me some water from the stream, for I should like to drink.'

'If you are thirsty,' said the waiting-maid, 'get off your horse yourself, and lie down and drink out of the water, I don't choose to be your servant.' So in her great thirst the princess alighted, bent down over the water in the stream and drank, and was not allowed to drink out of the golden cup. Then she said, 'Ah, Heaven!' and the three drops of blood answered, 'If thy mother knew, her heart would break.' But the King's daughter was humble, said nothing, and mounted her horse again.

She rode some miles further, but the day was warm, the sun scorched her, and she was thirsty once more, and when they came to a stream of water, she again cried to her waiting-maid, 'Dismount, and give me some water in my golden cup,' for she had long ago forgotten the girl's ill words. But the waiting-maid said still more haughtily, 'If you wish to drink, drink as you can, I don't choose to be your maid.' Then in her great thirst the King's daughter alighted, bent over the flowing stream, wept and said, 'Ah, Heaven!' and the drops of blood again replied, 'If thy mother knew this, her heart would break.' And as she was thus drinking and leaning right over the stream, the handkerchief with the three drops of blood fell out of her bosom, and floated away with the water without her observing it, so great was her trouble. The waiting-maid, however, had seen it, and she rejoiced to think that she now had power over the bride, for since the princess had lost the drops of blood, she had become weak and powerless. So now when she wanted to mount her horse again, the one that was called Falada, the waiting-maid said, 'Falada is more suitable for me, and my nag will do for thee,' and the princess had to be content with that. Then the waiting-maid, with many hard words, bade the princess exchange her royal apparel for her own shabby clothes; and at length she was compelled to swear by the clear sky above her that she would not say one word of this to anyone at the royal court, and if she had not taken this oath she would have been killed on the spot. But Falada saw all this, and observed it well.

The waiting-maid now mounted Falada, and the true bride the bad horse, and thus they travelled onwards, until at length they entered the royal palace. There were great rejoicings over her arrival, and the prince sprang forward to meet her, lifted the waiting-maid from her horse, and thought she was his consort. She was conducted upstairs, but the real princess was left standing below. Then the old King looked out of the window and saw her standing in the courtyard, and how dainty and delicate and beautiful she was, and instantly went to the royal apartment, and asked the bride about the girl she had with her who was standing down below in the courtyard, and who she was? 'I picked her up on my way for a companion; give the girl something to work at, that she may not stand idle.' But the old King had no work for her, and knew of none, so he said, 'I have a little boy who tends the geese, she may help him.'

The boy was called Conrad, and the true bride had to help him to tend the geese. Soon afterwards the false bride said to the young King, 'Dearest husband, I beg you to do me a favour.' He answered, 'I will do so most willingly.'

'Then send for the knacker, and have the head of the horse on which I rode here cut off, for it vexed me on the way.'

In reality, she was afraid that the horse might tell how she had behaved to the King's daughter. Then she succeeded in making the King promise that it should be done, and the faithful Falada was to die; this came to the ears of the real princess, and she secretly promised to pay the knacker a piece of gold if he would perform a small service for her. There was a great dark-looking gateway in the town, through which morning and evening she had to pass with the geese: would he be so good as to nail up Falada's head on it, so that she might see him again, more than once. The knacker's man promised to do that, and cut off the head, and nailed it fast beneath the dark gateway.

Early in the morning, when she and Conrad drove out their flock beneath this gateway, she said in passing,

> 'Alas, Falada, hanging there!'

Then the head answered,

> 'Alas, young Queen, how ill you fare!
> If this your tender mother knew,
> Her heart would surely break in two.'

Then they went still further out of the town, and drove their geese into the country. And when they had come to the meadow, she sat down and unbound her hair which was like pure gold, and Conrad saw it and delighted in its brightness, and wanted to pluck out a few hairs. Then she said,

> 'Blow, blow, thou gentle wind, I say,
> Blow Conrad's little hat away,
> And make him chase it here and there,
> Until I have braided all my hair,
> And bound it up again.'

And there came such a violent wind that it blew Conrad's hat far away across country, and he was forced to run after it. When he came back she had finished combing her hair and was putting it up again, and he could not get any of it. Then Conrad was angry, and would not speak to her, and thus they watched the geese until the evening, and then they went home.

Next day, when they were driving the geese out through the dark gateway, the maiden said,

'Alas, Falada, hanging there!'

Falada answered,

'Alas, young Queen, how ill you fare!
If this your tender mother knew,
Her heart would surely break in two.'

And she sat down again in the field and began to comb out her hair, and Conrad ran and tried to clutch it, so she said in haste,

'Blow, blow, thou gentle wind, I say,
Blow Conrad's little hat away,
And make him chase it here and there,
Until I have braided all my hair,
And bound it up again.'

Then the wind blew, and blew his little hat off his head and far away, and Conrad was forced to run after it, and when he came back, her hair had been put up a long time, and he could get none of it, and so they looked after their geese till evening came.

But in the evening after they had got home, Conrad went to the old King, and said, 'I won't tend the geese with that girl any longer!'

'Why not?' inquired the aged King.

'Oh, because she vexes me the whole day long.'

Then the aged King commanded him to relate what it was that she did to him. And Conrad said, 'In the morning when we pass beneath the dark gateway with the flock, there is a sorry horse's head on the wall, and she says to it,

"Alas, Falada, hanging there!"

And the head replies,

"Alas, young Queen how ill you fare!
If this your tender mother knew,
Her heart would surely break in two."'

And Conrad went on to relate what happened on the goose pasture, and how when there he had to chase his hat.

The aged King commanded him to drive his flock out again next day, and as soon as morning came, he placed himself behind the dark gateway, and heard how the maiden spoke to the head of Falada, and then he too went into the country, and hid himself in the thicket in the meadow. There he soon saw with his own eyes the goose-girl and the goose-boy bringing their flock, and how after a while she sat down and unplaited her hair, which shone with radiance. And soon she said,

'Blow, blow, thou gentle wind, I say,
Blow Conrad's little hat away,
And make him chase it here and there,
Until I have braided all my hair,

THE GOOSE-GIRL

And bound it up again.'

Then came a blast of wind and carried off Conrad's hat, so that he had to run far away, while the maiden quietly went on combing and plaiting her hair, all of which the King observed. Then, quite unseen, he went away, and when the goose-girl came home in the evening, he called her aside, and asked why she did all these things. 'I may not tell you that, and I dare not lament my sorrows to any human being, for I have sworn not to do so by the heaven which is above me; if I had not done that, I should have lost my life.' He urged her and left her no peace, but he could draw nothing from her. Then said he, 'If thou wilt not tell me anything, tell thy sorrows to the iron-stove there,' and he went away. Then she crept into the iron-stove, and began to weep and lament, and emptied her whole heart, and said, 'Here am I deserted by the whole world, and yet I am a King's daughter, and a false waiting-maid has by force brought me to such a pass that I have been compelled to put off my royal apparel, and she has taken my place with my bridegroom, and I have to perform menial service as a goose-girl. If my mother did but know that, her heart would break.'

The aged King, however, was standing outside by the pipe of the stove, and was listening to what she said, and heard it. Then he came back again, and bade her come out of the stove. And royal garments were placed on her, and it was marvellous how beautiful she was! The aged King summoned his son, and revealed to him that he had got the false bride who was only a waiting-maid, but that the true one was standing there, as the sometime goose-girl.

The young King rejoiced with all his heart when he saw her beauty and youth, and a great feast was made ready to which all the people and all good friends were invited. At the head of the table sat the bridegroom with the King's daughter at one side of him, and the waiting-maid on the other, but the waiting-maid was blinded, and did not recognize the princess in her dazzling array. When they had eaten and drunk, and were merry, the aged King asked the waiting-maid as a riddle, what a person deserved who had behaved in such and such a way to her master, and at the same time related the whole story, and asked what sentence such an one merited? Then the false bride said, 'She deserves no better fate than to be stripped entirely naked, and put in a barrel which is studded inside with pointed nails, and two white horses should be harnessed to it, which will drag her along through one street after another, till she is dead.'

'It is thou,' said the aged King, 'and thou hast pronounced thine own sentence, and thus shall it be done unto thee.'

And when the sentence had been carried out, the young King married his true bride, and both of them reigned over their kingdom in peace and happiness.

THE KING OF THE GOLDEN MOUNTAIN

There was a certain merchant who had two children, a boy and a girl; they were both young, and could not walk. And two richly laden ships of his sailed forth to sea with all his property on board, and just as he was expecting to win much money by them, news came that they had gone to the bottom, and now instead of being a rich man he was a poor one, and had nothing left but one field outside the town. In order to drive his misfortune a little out of his thoughts, he went out to this field, and as he was walking forwards and backwards in it, a little black mannikin stood suddenly by his side, and asked why he was so sad, and what he was taking so much to heart. Then said the merchant, 'If thou couldst help me I would willingly tell thee.'

'Who knows?' replied the black dwarf. 'Perhaps, I can help thee.'

Then the merchant told him that all he possessed had gone to the bottom of the sea, and that he had nothing left but this field.

'Do not trouble thyself,' said the dwarf. 'If thou wilt promise to give me the first thing that rubs itself against thy leg when thou art at home again, and to bring it here to this place in twelve years' time, thou shalt have as much money as thou wilt.'

The merchant thought, 'What can that be but my dog?' and did not remember his little boy, so he said yes, gave the black man a written and sealed promise, and went home.

When he reached home, his little boy was so delighted that

he held by a bench, tottered up to him and seized him fast by the legs. The father was shocked, for he remembered his promise, and now knew what he had pledged himself to do; as however, he still found no money in his chest, he thought the dwarf had only been jesting. A month afterwards he went up to the garret, intending to gather together some old tin and to sell it, and saw a great heap of money lying there. Then he was happy again, made purchases, became a greater merchant than before, and felt that this world was well-governed. In the meantime the boy grew tall, and at the same time sharp and clever. But the nearer the twelfth year approached the more anxious grew the merchant, so that his distress might be seen in his face.

One day his son asked what ailed him, but the father would not say. The boy, however, persisted so long, that at last he told him that without being aware of what he was doing, he had promised him to a black dwarf, and had received much money for doing so. He said likewise that he had set his hand and seal to this, and that now when twelve years had gone by he would have to give him up. Then said the son, 'Oh, father, do not be uneasy, all will go well. The black man has no power over me.' The son had himself blessed by the priest, and when the time came, father and son went together to the field, and the son made a circle and placed himself inside it with his father. Then came the black dwarf and said to the old man, 'Hast thou brought with thee that which thou hast promised me?'

He was silent, but the son asked, 'What dost thou want here?'

Then said the black dwarf, 'I have to speak with thy father, and not with thee.'

The son replied, 'Thou hast betrayed and misled my father, give back the writing.'

'No,' said the black dwarf, 'I will not give up my rights.'

They spoke together for a long time after this, but at last they agreed that the son, as he did not belong to the enemy of mankind, nor yet to his father, should seat himself in a small boat, which should lie on water which was flowing away from them, and that the father should push it off with his own foot, and then the son should remain given up to the water. So he took leave of his father, placed himself in a little boat, and the father had to push it off with his own foot. The boat capsized so that the keel was uppermost, and the father believed his son was lost, and went home and mourned for him.

The boat, however, did not sink, but floated quietly away, and the boy sat safely inside it, and it floated thus for a long time, until at last it stopped by an unknown shore. Then he landed and saw a beautiful castle before him, and set out to go to it. But when he entered it, he found that it was bewitched. He went through every room, but all were empty until he reached the last, where a snake lay coiled in a ring. The snake, however, was an enchanted maiden, who rejoiced to see him, and said, 'Hast thou come, oh, my deliverer? I have already waited twelve years for thee; this kingdom is bewitched, and thou must set it free.'

'How can I do that?' he inquired.

'Tonight come twelve black men, covered with chains, who will ask what thou art doing here; keep silent; give them no answer, and let them do what they will with thee; they will torment thee, beat thee, stab thee; let everything pass, only do not speak; at twelve o'clock, they must go away again. On the second night twelve others will come; on the third, four-and-twenty, who will cut off thy head, but at twelve o'clock their power will be over, and then if thou hast endured all, and hast not spoken the slightest word, I shall be released. I will come to thee, and will have, in a bottle, some of the water of life. I will rub thee with that, and then thou wilt come to life again, and be as healthy as before.'

Then said he, 'I will gladly set thee free.'

And everything happened just as she had said; the black men could not force a single word from him, and on the third night the snake became a beautiful princess, who came with the water of life and brought him back to life again. So she threw herself into his arms and kissed him, and there was joy and gladness in the whole castle. After this their marriage was celebrated, and he was King of the Golden Mountain.

They lived very happily together, and the Queen bore a fine boy. Eight years had already gone by, when the King bethought him of his father; his heart was moved, and he wished to visit him. The Queen, however, would not let him go away, and said, 'I know beforehand that it will cause my unhappiness'; but he suffered her to have no rest until she consented. At their parting she gave him a wishing-ring, and said, 'Take this ring and put it on thy finger, and then thou wilt immediately be transported whithersoever thou wouldst be, only thou must promise me not to use it in wishing me away from this place and with thy father.'

That he promised her, put the ring on his finger, and wished himself at home, just outside the town where his father lived. Instantly, he found himself there, and made for the town, but when he came to the gate, the sentries would not let him in, because he wore such strange and yet such rich and magnificent clothing. Then he went to a hill where a shepherd was watching his sheep, changed clothes with him, put on his old shepherd's-coat, and then entered the town without hindrance. When he came to his father, he made himself known to him, but he did not at

THE KING OF THE GOLDEN MOUNTAIN

all believe that the shepherd was his son, and said he certainly had had a son, but that he was dead long ago; however, as he saw he was a poor, needy shepherd, he would give him something to eat. Then the shepherd said to his parents, 'I am verily your son. Do you know of no mark on my body by which you could recognize me?'

'Yes,' said his mother, 'our son had a raspberry mark under his right arm.'

He slipped back his shirt, and they saw the raspberry under his right arm, and no longer doubted that he was their son. Then he told them that he was King of the Golden Mountain, and a king's daughter was his wife, and that they had a fine son of seven years old. Then said the father, 'That is certainly not true; it is a fine kind of a king who goes about in a ragged shepherd's-coat.' On this the son fell in a passion, and without thinking of his promise, turned his ring round, and wished both his wife and child with him. They were there in a second, but the Queen wept, and reproached him, and said that he had broken his word, and had brought misfortune upon her. He said, 'I have done it thoughtlessly, and not with evil intention,' and tried to calm her, and she pretended to believe this; but she had mischief in her mind.

Then he led her out of the town into the field, and showed her the stream where the little boat had been pushed off, and then he said, 'I am tired; sit down, I will sleep awhile on thy lap.' And he laid his head on her lap, and fell asleep. When he was asleep, she first drew the ring from his finger, then she drew away the foot which was under him, leaving only the slipper behind her, and she took her child in her arms, and wished herself back in her own kingdom.

When he awoke, there he lay quite deserted, and his wife and child were gone, and so was the ring from his finger, the slipper only was still there as a token. 'Home to thy parents thou canst not return,' thought he, 'they would say that thou wast a wizard; thou must be off, and walk on until thou arrives in thine own kingdom.'

So he went away and came at length to a hill by which three giants were standing, disputing with each other because they did not know how to divide their father's property. When they saw him passing by, they called to him and said little men had quick wits, and that he was to divide their inheritance for them. The inheritance, however, consisted of a sword, which had this property that if any one took it in his hand, and said, 'All heads off but mine,' every head would lie on the ground; secondly, of a cloak which made any one who put it on invisible; thirdly, of a pair of boots which could transport the wearer to any place he wished in a moment.

He said, 'Give me the three things that I may see if they are still in good condition.' They gave him the cloak, and when he had put it on, he was invisible and changed into a fly. Then he resumed his own form and said, 'The cloak is a good one, now give me the sword.' They said, 'No, we will not give thee that; if thou were to say, "All heads off but mine," all our heads would be off, and thou alone wouldst be left with thine.'

Nevertheless they gave it to him with the condition that he was only to try it against a tree. This he did, and the sword cut in two the trunk of a tree as if it had been a blade of straw.

Then he wanted to have the boots likewise, but they said, 'No, we will not give them; if thou hadst them on thy feet and wert to wish thyself at the top of the hill, we should be left down here with nothing.'

'Oh, no,' said he, 'I will not do that.'

So they gave him the boots as well. And now when he had got all these things, he thought of nothing but his wife and his child, and said as though to himself, 'Oh, if I were but on the Golden Mountain,' and at the same moment he vanished from the sight of the giants, and thus their inheritance was divided. When he was near his palace, he heard sounds of joy, and fiddles, and flutes, and the people told him that his wife was celebrating her wedding with another. Then he fell into a rage, and said, 'False woman, she betrayed and deserted me whilst I was asleep!' So he put on his cloak, and unseen by all went into the palace. When he entered the dining-hall, a great table was spread with delicious food, and the guests were eating and drinking, and laughing, and jesting. She sat on a royal seat in the midst of them in splendid apparel, with a crown on her head. He placed himself behind her, and no one saw him. When she put a piece of meat on a plate for herself, he took it away and ate it, and when she poured out a glass of wine for herself, he took it away and drank it. She was always helping herself to something, and yet she never got anything, for plate and glass disappeared immediately. Then dismayed and ashamed, she arose and went to her chamber and wept, but he followed her there. She said, 'Has the devil power over me, or did my deliverer never come?'

Then he struck her in the face, and said, 'Did thy deliverer never come? It is he who has thee in his power, thou traitor. Have I deserved this from thee?' Then he made himself visible, went into the hall, and cried, 'The wedding is at an end, the true King has returned.' The kings, princes, and councillors who were assembled there, ridiculed and mocked him, but he did not trouble to answer them, and said, 'Will you go away, or not?' On this, they tried to seize him and pressed upon him, but he drew his sword and said, 'All heads off but mine,' and all the heads rolled on the ground, and he alone was master, and once more King of the Golden Mountain.

THE PEASANT'S WISE DAUGHTER

There was once a poor peasant who had no land, but only a small house, and one daughter. Then said the daughter, 'We ought to ask our lord the King for a bit of newly cleared land.' When the King heard of their poverty, he presented them with a piece of land, which she and her father dug up, and intended to sow with a little corn and grain of that kind. When they had dug nearly the whole of the field, they found in the earth a mortar made of pure gold. 'Listen,' said the father to the girl, 'as our lord the King has been so gracious and presented us with the field, we ought to give him this mortar in return for it.' The daughter, however, would not consent to this, and said, 'Father, if we have the mortar without having the pestle as well, we shall have to get the pestle, so you had much better say nothing about it.' He would, however, not obey her, but took the mortar and carried it to the King, said that he had found it in the cleared land, and asked if he would accept it as a present. The King took the mortar, and asked if he had found nothing besides that? 'No,' answered the countryman. Then the King said that he must now bring him the pestle. The peasant said they had not found that, but he might just as well have spoken to the wind; he was put in prison, and was to stay there until he produced the pestle.

The servants had daily to carry him bread and water, which is what people get in prison, and they heard how the man cried out continually, 'Ah! if I had but listened to my daughter! Alas, alas, if I had but listened to my daughter!' Then the servants went to the King and told him how the prisoner was always crying, 'Ah! if I had but listened to my daughter!' and would neither eat nor drink. So he commanded the servants to bring the prisoner before him, and then the King asked the peasant why he was always crying, 'Ah! If I had but listened to my daughter!' and what it was that his daughter had said. 'She told me that I ought not to take the mortar to you, for I should have to produce the pestle as well.'

'If you have a daughter who is as wise as that, let her come here.' She was therefore obliged to appear before the King, who asked her if she really was so wise, and said he would set her a riddle, and if she could guess that, he would marry her. She at once said yes, she would guess it. Then said the King, 'Come to me not clothed, not naked, not riding, not walking, not in the road, and not out of the road, and if thou canst do that I will marry thee.' So she went away, put off everything she had on, and then she was not clothed, and took a great fishing net, and seated herself in it and wrapped it entirely round and round her, so that she was not naked, and she hired an ass, and tied the fisherman's net to its tail, so that it was forced to drag her along, and that was neither riding nor walking. The ass had also to drag her in the ruts, so that she only touched the ground with her great toe, and that was neither being in the road nor out of the road. And when she arrived in that fashion, the King said she had guessed the riddle and fulfilled all the conditions. Then he ordered her father to be released from the prison, took her to wife, and gave into her care all the royal possessions.

Now when some years had passed, the King was once

drawing up his troops on parade, when it happened that some peasants who had been selling wood stopped with their waggons before the palace; some of them had oxen yoked to them, and some horses. There was one peasant who had three horses, one of which was delivered of a young foal, and it ran away and lay down between two oxen which were in front of the waggon. When the peasants came together, they began to dispute, to beat each other and make a disturbance, and the peasant with the oxen wanted to keep the foal, and said one of the oxen had given birth to it, and the other said his horse had had it, and that it was his. The quarrel came before the King, and he give the verdict that the foal should stay where it had been found, and so the peasant with the oxen, to whom it did not belong, got it. Then the other went away, and wept and lamented over his foal.

Now he had heard how gracious his lady the Queen was because she herself had sprung from poor peasant folks, so he went to her and begged her to see if she could not help him to get his foal back again. Said she, 'Yes, I will tell you what to do, if thou wilt promise me not to betray me. Early tomorrow morning, when the King parades the guard, place thyself there in the middle of the road by which he must pass, take a great fishing-net and pretend to be fishing; go on fishing, too, and empty out the net as if thou hadst got it full' – and then she told him also what he was to say if he was questioned by the King.

The next day, therefore, the peasant stood there, and fished on dry ground. When the King passed by, and saw that, he sent his messenger to ask what the stupid man was about? He answered, 'I am fishing.' The messenger asked how he could fish when there was no water there? The peasant said, 'It is as easy for me to fish on dry land as it is for an ox to have a foal.' The messenger went back and took the answer to the King, who ordered the peasant to be brought to him and told him that this was not his own idea, and he wanted to know whose it was? The peasant must confess this at once. The peasant, however, would not do so, and said always, God forbid he should! the idea was his own. They laid him, however, on a heap of straw, and beat him and tormented him so long that at last he admitted that he had got the idea from the Queen.

When the King reached home again, he said to his wife, 'Why hast thou behaved so falsely to me? I will not have thee any longer for a wife; thy time is up, go back to the place from whence thou camest – to thy peasant's hut.' One favour, however, he granted her; she might take with her the one thing that was dearest and best in her eyes; and thus was she dismissed. She said, 'Yes, my dear husband, if you command this, I will do it,' and she embraced him and kissed him, and said she would take leave of him.

Then she ordered a powerful sleeping draught to be brought, to drink farewell to him; the King took a long draught, but she took only a little. He soon fell into a deep sleep, and when she perceived that, she called a servant and took a fair white linen cloth and wrapped the King in it, and the servant was forced to carry him into a carriage that stood before the door, and she drove with him to her own little house. She laid him in her own little bed, and he slept one day and one night without awakening, and when he awoke he looked round and said, 'Good God! where am I?' He called his attendants, but none of them were there. At length his wife came to his bedside and said, 'My dear lord and King, you told me I might bring away with me from the palace that which was dearest and most precious in my eyes. I have nothing more precious and dear than yourself, so I have brought you with me.' Tears rose to the King's eyes and he said, 'Dear wife, thou shalt be mine and I will be thine,' and he took her back with him to the royal palace and was married again to her, and at the present time they are very likely still living.

THE DEVIL'S SOOTY BROTHER

A disbanded soldier had nothing to live on, and did not know how to get on. So he went out into the forest and when he had walked for a short time, he met a little man who was, however, the Devil. The little man said to him, 'What ails you, you seem so very sorrowful?'

Then the soldier said, 'I am hungry, but have no money.'

The Devil said, 'If you will hire yourself to me, and be my serving-man, you shall have enough for all your life. You shall serve me for seven years, and after that you shall again be free. But one thing I must tell you, and that is, you must not wash, comb, or trim yourself, or cut your hair or nails, or wipe the water from your eyes.'

The soldier said, 'All right, if there is no help for it,' and went off with the little man, who straightway led him down into hell. Then he told him what he had to do. He was to poke the fire under the kettles wherein the hell-broth was stewing, keep the house clean, drive all the sweepings behind the doors, and see that everything was in order, but if he once peeped into the kettles, it would go ill with him.

The soldier said, 'Good, I will take care.' And then the old Devil went out again on his wanderings, and the soldier entered upon his new duties, made the fire, and swept the dirt well behind the doors, just as he had been bidden. When the old Devil came back again, he looked to see if all had been done, appeared satisfied, and went forth a second time. The soldier now took a good look on every side; the kettles were standing all round hell with a mighty fire below them, and inside they were boiling and sputtering. He would have given anything to look inside them, if the Devil had not so particularly forbidden him: at last, he could no longer restrain himself, slightly raised the lid of the first kettle, and peeped in, and there he saw his former corporal shut in. 'Aha, old bird!' said he, 'Do I meet you here? You once had me in your power, now I have you,' and he quickly let the lid fall, poked the fire, and added a fresh log. After that, he went to the second kettle, raised its lid also a little, and peeped in; his former ensign was in that. 'Aha, old bird, so I find you here! you once had me in your power, now I have you.' He closed the lid again, and fetched yet another log to make it really hot. Then he wanted to see who might be sitting up in the third kettle. It was actually a general. 'Aha, old bird, do I meet you here? Once you had me in your power, now I have you.' And he fetched the bellows and made hell-fire blaze right under him.

So he did his work seven years in hell, did not wash, comb, or trim himself, or cut his hair or nails, or wash the water out of his eyes, and the seven years seemed so short to him that he thought he had only been half a year. Now when the time had fully gone by, the Devil came and said, 'Well, Hans, what have you done?'

'I poked the fire under the kettles, and I have swept all the dirt well behind the doors.'

'But you have peeped into the kettles as well; it is lucky for you that you added fresh logs to them, or else your life would have been forfeited; now that your time is up, will you go home again?'

'Yes,' said the soldier, 'I should very much like to see what my father is doing at home.'

The Devil said, 'In order that you may receive the wages you have earned, go and fill your knapsack full of the sweepings, and take it home with you. You must also go unwashed and uncombed, with long hair on your head and beard, and with uncut nails and dim eyes, and when you are asked whence you come, you must say, "From hell," and when you are asked who you are, you are to say, "The Devil's sooty brother, and my King as well."'

The soldier held his peace, and did as the Devil bade him, but he was not at all satisfied with his wages. Then as soon as he was up in the forest again, he took his knapsack from his back, to empty it, but on opening it, the sweepings had become pure gold. 'I should never have expected that,' said he, and was well pleased, and entered the town. The landlord was standing in front of the inn, and when he saw the soldier approaching, he was terrified, because Hans looked so horrible, worse than a scarecrow. He called to him and asked, 'Whence comest thou?'

'From hell.'

'Who art thou?'

'The Devil's sooty brother, and my King as well.' Then the host would not let him enter, but when Hans showed him the gold, he came and unlatched the door himself. Hans then ordered the best room and attendance, ate, and drank his fill, but neither washed nor combed himself as the Devil had bidden him, and at last lay down to sleep. But the knapsack full of gold remained before the eyes of the landlord, and left him no peace, and during the night he crept in and stole it away. Next morning, however, when Hans got up and wanted to pay the landlord and travel further, behold his knapsack was gone! But he soon composed himself and thought, 'Thou hast been unfortunate from no fault of thine own,' and straightway went back again to hell, complained of his misfortune to the old Devil, and begged for his help.

The Devil said, 'Seat yourself, I will wash, comb, and trim you, cut your hair and nails, and wash your eyes for you,' and when he had done with him, he gave him the knapsack back again full of sweepings, and said, 'Go and tell the landlord that he must return you your money, or else I will come and fetch him, and he shall poke the fire in your place.'

Hans went up and said to the landlord, 'Thou hast stolen my money; if thou dost not return it, thou shalt go down to hell in my place, and wilt look as horrible as I.' Then the landlord gave him the money, and more besides, only begging him to keep it secret, and Hans was now a rich man.

He set out on his way home to his father, bought himself a shabby smock-frock to wear, and strolled about making music, for he had learned to do that while he was with the Devil in hell. There was however, an old King in that country, before whom he had to play, and the King was so delighted with his playing, that he promised him his eldest daughter in marriage. But when she heard that she was to be married to a common fellow in a smock-frock, she said, 'Rather than do that, I would go into the deepest water.' Then the King gave him the youngest, who was quite willing to do it to please her father, and thus the Devil's sooty brother got the King's daughter, and when the aged King died, the whole kingdom likewise.

BEARSKIN

There was once a young fellow who enlisted as a soldier, conducted himself bravely, and was always the foremost when it rained bullets. So long as the war lasted, all went well, but when peace was made, he received his dismissal, and the captain said he might go where he liked. His parents were dead, and he had no longer a home, so he went to his brothers and begged them to take him in, and keep him until war broke out again. The brothers, however, were hard-hearted and said, 'What can we do with thee? Thou art of no use to us; go and make a living for thyself.'

The soldier had nothing left but his gun; he took that on his shoulder, and went forth into the world. He came to a wide heath, on which nothing was to be seen but a circle of trees; under these he sat sorrowfully down, and began to think over his fate. 'I have no money,' thought he, 'I have learnt no trade but that of fighting, and now that they have made peace they don't want me any longer; so I see beforehand that I shall have to starve.'

All at once he heard a rustling, and when he looked round, a strange man stood before him, who wore a green coat and looked right stately, but had a hideous cloven foot. 'I know already what thou art in need of,' said the man; 'gold and possessions shalt thou have, as much as thou canst make away with do what thou wilt, but first I must know if thou art fearless, that I may not bestow my money in vain.'

'A soldier and fear – how can those two things go together?' he answered; 'thou canst put me to the proof.'

'Very well, then,' answered the man, 'look behind thee.'

The soldier turned round, and saw a large bear, which came growling towards him. 'Oho!' cried the soldier, 'I will tickle thy nose for thee, so that thou shalt soon lose thy fancy for growling,' and he aimed at the bear and shot it through the muzzle; it fell down and never stirred again.

'I see quite well,' said the stranger, 'that thou art not wanting in courage, but there is still another condition which thou wilt have to fulfil.'

'If it does not endanger my salvation,' replied the soldier, who knew very well who was standing by him. 'If it does, I'll have nothing to do with it.'

'Thou wilt look to that for thyself,' answered Greencoat; 'thou shalt for the next seven years neither wash thyself, nor comb thy beard, nor thy hair, nor cut thy nails, nor say one paternoster. I will give thee a coat and a cloak, which during this time thou must wear. If thou diest during these seven years, thou art mine; if thou remainest alive, thou art free, and rich to boot, for all the rest of thy life.' The soldier thought of the great extremity in which he now found himself, and as he so often had gone to meet death, he resolved to risk it now also, and agreed to the terms. The Devil took off his green coat, gave it to the soldier, and said, 'If thou hast this coat on thy back and puttest thy hand into the pocket, thou wilt always find it full of money.' Then he pulled the skin off the bear and said, 'This shall be thy cloak, and thy bed also, for thereon shalt thou sleep, and in no other bed shalt thou lie, and because of this apparel shalt thou be called Bearskin.' After this the Devil vanished.

The soldier put the coat on, felt at once in the pocket, and found that the thing was really true. Then he put on the bearskin and went forth into the world, and enjoyed himself, refraining from nothing that did him good and his money harm. During the first year, his appearance was passable, but during the second he began to look like a monster. His hair covered nearly the whole of his face, his beard was like a piece of coarse felt, his fingers had claws, and his face was so covered with dirt that if cress had been sown on it, it would have come up. Whosoever saw him, ran away, but as he everywhere gave the poor money to pray that he might not die during the seven years, and as he paid well for everything he still always found shelter.

In the fourth year, he entered an inn where the landlord would not receive him, and would not even let him have a place in the stable, because he was afraid the horses would be scared. But as Bearskin thrust his hand into his pocket and pulled out a handful of ducats, the host let himself be persuaded and gave him a room in an outhouse. Bearskin was, however, obliged to promise not to let himself be seen, lest the inn should get a bad name.

As Bearskin was sitting alone in the evening, and wishing from the bottom of his heart that the seven years were over, he heard a loud lamenting in a neighbouring room. He had a compassionate heart, so he opened the door, and saw an old man weeping bitterly, and wringing his hands. Bearskin went nearer, but the man sprang to his feet and tried to escape from him. At last when the man perceived that Bearskin's voice was human, he let himself be prevailed on, and by kind words Bearskin succeeded so far that the old man revealed the cause of his grief. His property had dwindled away by degrees, he and his daughters would have to starve, and he was so poor that he could not pay the innkeeper, and was to be put in prison. 'If that is your only trouble,' said Bearskin, 'I have plenty of money.' He caused the innkeeper to be brought thither, paid him and put a purse full of gold into the poor old man's pocket besides.

When the old man saw himself set free from all his troubles he did not know how to be grateful enough. 'Come with me,' said he to Bearskin; 'my daughters are all miracles of beauty, choose one of them for thyself as a wife. When she hears what thou hast done for me, she will not refuse thee. Thou dost in truth look a little strange, but she will soon put thee to rights again.' This pleased Bearskin well, and he went. When the eldest saw him she was so terribly alarmed at his face that she screamed and ran away.

The second stood still and looked at him from head to foot, but then she said, 'How can I accept a husband who no longer has a human form? The shaven bear that once was here and passed itself off for a man pleased me far better, for at any rate it wore a hussar's dress and white gloves. If it were nothing but ugliness, I might get used to that.'

The youngest, however, said, 'Dear father, that must be a good man to have helped you out of your trouble, so if you have promised him a bride for doing it, your promise must be kept.' It was a pity that Bearskin's face was covered with dirt and with hair, for if not they might have seen how delighted he was when he heard these words. He took a ring from his finger, broke it in two, and gave her one half, the other he kept for himself. He wrote his name, however, on her half, and hers on his, and begged her to keep her piece carefully, and then he took his leave and said, 'I must still wander about for three years, and if I do not return then, thou art free, for I shall be dead. But pray to God to preserve my life.'

The poor betrothed bride dressed herself entirely in black, and when she thought of her future bridegroom, tears came into her eyes. Nothing but contempt and mockery fell to her lot from her sisters. 'Take care,' said the eldest, 'if thou givest him thy hand, he will strike his claws into it.'

'Beware!' said the second. 'Bears like sweet things, and if he takes a fancy to thee, he will eat thee up.'

'Thou must always do as he likes,' began the elder again, 'or else he will growl.'

And the second continued, 'But the wedding will be a merry one, for bears dance well.'

The bride was silent, and did not let them vex her. Bearskin, however, travelled about the world from one place to another, did good where he was able, and gave generously to the poor that they might pray for him.

At length, as the last day of the seven years dawned, he went once more out on to the heath, and seated himself beneath the circle of trees. It was not long before the wind whistled, and the Devil stood before him and looked angrily at him; then he threw Bearskin his old coat, and asked for his own green one back. 'We have not got so far as that yet,' answered Bearskin, 'thou must first make me clean.' Whether the Devil liked it or not, he was forced to fetch water, and wash Bearskin, comb his hair, and cut his nails. After this, he looked like a brave soldier, and was much handsomer than he had ever been before.

When the Devil had gone away, Bearskin was quite light-hearted. He went into the town, put on a magnificent velvet coat, seated himself in a carriage drawn by four white horses, and drove to his bride's house. No one recognized him, the father took him for a distinguished general, and led him into the room where his daughters were sitting. He was forced to place himself between the two eldest, they helped him to wine, gave him the best pieces of meat, and thought that in all the world they had never seen a handsomer man. The bride, however, sat opposite to him in her black dress, and never raised her eyes, nor spoke a word.

When at length he asked the father if he would give him one of his daughters to wife, the two eldest jumped up, ran into their bedrooms to put on splendid dresses, for each of them fancied she was the chosen one. The stranger, as soon as he was alone with his bride, brought out his half of the ring, and threw it in a glass of wine which he reached across the table to her. She took the wine, but when she had drunk it, and found the half ring lying at the bottom, her heart began to beat. She got the other half, which she wore on a ribbon round her neck, joined them, and saw that the two pieces fitted exactly together.

Then said he, 'I am thy betrothed bridegroom, whom thou sawest as Bearskin, but through God's grace I have again received my human form, and have once more become clean.' He went up to her, embraced her, and gave her a kiss. In the meantime the two sisters came back in full dress, and when they saw that the handsome man had fallen to the share of the youngest, and heard that he was Bearskin, they ran out full of anger and rage. One of them drowned herself in the well, the other hanged herself on a tree. In the evening, someone knocked at the door, and when the bridegroom opened it, it was the Devil in his green coat, who said, 'Seest thou, I have now got two souls in the place of thy one!'

THE THREE ARMY SURGEONS

Three army surgeons who thought they knew their art perfectly, were travelling about the world, and they came to an inn where they wanted to pass the night. The host asked whence they came, and whither they were going? 'We are roaming about the world and practising our art.'

'Just show me for once in a way what you can do,' said the host. Then the first said he would cut off his hand, and put it on again early next morning; the second said he would tear out his heart, and replace it next morning; the third said he would cut out his eyes and heal them again next morning.

'If you can do that,' said the innkeeper, 'you have learnt everything.'

They, however, had a salve, with which they rubbed themselves, which joined parts together, and they carried the little bottle in which it was, constantly with them. Then they cut the hand, heart and eyes from their bodies as they had said they would, and laid them all together on a plate, and gave it to the innkeeper. The innkeeper gave it to a servant who was to set it in the cupboard, and take good care of it. The girl, however, had a lover in secret, who was a soldier. When therefore the innkeeper, the three army-surgeons, and everyone else in the house were asleep, the soldier came and wanted something to eat. The girl opened the cupboard and brought him some food, and in her love forgot to shut the cupboard door again; she seated herself at the table by her lover,

THE THREE ARMY SURGEONS

and they chattered away together. While she sat so contentedly there, thinking of no ill luck, the cat came creeping in, found the cupboard open, took the hand and heart and eyes of the three army-surgeons, and ran off with them.

When the soldier had done eating, and the girl was taking away the things and going to shut the cupboard she saw that the plate which the innkeeper had given her to take care of, was empty. Then she said in a fright to her lover, 'Ah, miserable girl, what shall I do? The hand is gone, the heart and the eyes are gone too, what will become of me in the morning?'

'Be easy,' said he, 'I will help thee out of thy trouble: there is a thief hanging outside on the gallows, I will cut off his hand. Which hand was it?'

'The right one.' Then the girl gave him a sharp knife, and he went and cut the poor sinner's right hand off, and brought it to her. After this he caught the cat and cut its eyes out, and now nothing but the heart was wanting. 'Have you not been killing, and are not the dead pigs in the cellar?' said he.

'Yes,' said the girl.

'That's well,' said the soldier, and he went down and fetched a pig's heart. The girl placed all together on the plate, and put it in the cupboard, and when after this her lover took leave of her, she went quietly to bed.

In the morning when the three army surgeons got up, they told the girl she was to bring them the plate on which the hand, heart, and eyes were lying. Then she brought it out of the cupboard, and the first fixed the thief's hand on and smeared it with his salve, and it grew to his arm directly. The second took the cat's eyes and put them in his own head. The third fixed the pig's heart firm in the place where his own had been, and the innkeeper stood by, admired their skill, and said he had never yet seen such a thing as that done, and would sing their praises and recommend them to everyone. Then they paid their bill, and travelled farther.

As they were on their way, the one with the pig's heart did not stay with them at all, but wherever there was a corner he ran to it, and rooted about in it with his nose as pigs do. The others wanted to hold him back by the tail of his coat, but that did no good; he tore himself loose, and ran wherever the dirt was thickest. The second also behaved very strangely; he rubbed his eyes, and said to the others, 'Comrades, what is the matter? I don't see at all. Will one of you lead me, so that I do not fall.'

Then with difficulty they travelled on till evening, when they reached another inn. They went into the bar together, and there at a table in the corner sat a rich man counting money. The one with the thief's hand walked round about him, made a sudden movement twice with his arm, and at last when the stranger turned away, he snatched at the pile of money, and took a handful from it. One of them saw this, and said, 'Comrade, what art thou about? Thou must not steal – shame on thee!'

'Eh,' said he, 'but how can I stop myself? My hand twitches, and I am forced to snatch things whether I will or not.'

After this, they lay down to sleep, and while they were lying there it was so dark that no one could see his own hand. All at once, the one with the cat's eyes awoke, aroused the others, and said. 'Brothers, just look up, do you see the white mice running about there?' The two sat up, but could see nothing. Then said he, 'Things are not right with us, we have not got back again what is ours. We must return to the innkeeper, he has deceived us.'

They went back, therefore, the next morning, and told the host they had not got what was their own again; that the first had a thief's hand, the second cat's eyes, and the third a pig's heart. The innkeeper said that the girl must be to blame for that, and was going to call her, but when she had seen the three coming, she had run out by the backdoor, and not come back. Then the three said he must give them a great deal of money, or they would set his house on fire[1]. He gave them what he had, and whatever he could get together, and the three went away with it. It was enough for the rest of their lives, but they would rather have had their own proper organs.

---

[1] 'Sonst liessen sie ihm den rothen Hahn übers Haus fliegen.' The symbol of a red cock for fire is of remote antiquity. 'I will set a red cock on your roof' is the incendiary's threat in Germany, where fire is compared to a cock flying from house to house.

THE SEVEN SWABIANS

Seven Swabians were once together. The first was Master Schulz; the second, Jackli; the third, Marli; the fourth, Jergli; the fifth, Michal; the sixth, Hans; the seventh, Veitli: all seven had made up their minds to travel about the world to seek adventures, and perform great deeds. But in order that they might go in security and with arms in their hands, they thought it would be advisable that they should have one solitary, but very strong, and very long spear made for them. This spear all seven of them took in their hands at once; in front walked the boldest and bravest, and that was Master Schulz; all the others followed in a row, and Veitli was the last. Then it came to pass one day in the hay-making month (July), when they had walked a long distance, and still had a long way to go before they reached the village where they were to pass the night, that as they were in a meadow in the twilight a great beetle or hornet flew by them from behind a bush, and hummed in a menacing manner. Master Schulz was so terrified that he all but dropped the spear, and a cold perspiration broke out over his whole body.

'Hark! hark!' cried he to his comrades, 'Good heavens! I hear a drum.'

Jackli, who was behind him holding the spear, and who perceived some kind of a smell, said, 'Something is most certainly going on, for I taste powder and matches.' At these words Master Schulz began to take to flight, and in a trice jumped over a hedge, but as he just happened to jump onto the teeth of a rake which had been left lying there after the hay-making, the handle of it struck against his face and gave him a tremendous blow. 'Oh dear! Oh dear!' screamed Master Schulz. 'Take me prisoner; I surrender! I surrender!' The other six all leapt over, one on the top of the other, crying, 'If you surrender, I surrender too! If you surrender, I surrender too!' At length, as no enemy was there to bind and take them away, they saw that they had been mistaken, and in order that the story might not be known, and they be treated as fools and ridiculed, they all swore to each other to hold their peace about it until one of them accidentally spoke of it. Then they journeyed onwards.

The second danger which they survived cannot be compared with the first. Some days afterwards, their path led them through a fallow field where a hare was sitting sleeping in the sun. Her ears were standing straight up, and her great glassy eyes were wide open. All of them were alarmed at the sight of the horrible wild beast, and they consulted together as to what it would be the least dangerous to do. For if they were to run away, they knew that the monster would pursue and swallow them whole. So they said, 'We must go through a great and dangerous struggle. Boldly ventured, is half won,' and all seven grasped the spear, Master Schulz in front, and Veitli behind. Master Schulz was always trying to keep the spear back, but Veitli had become quite brave while behind, and wanted to dash forward and cried,

'Strike home, in every Swabian's name,
Or else I wish ye may be lame.'

But Hans knew how to meet this, and said,

> 'Thunder and lightning, it's fine to prate,
> But for dragon-hunting thou'rt aye too late.'

Michal cried,

> 'Nothing is wanting, not even a hair,
> Be sure the Devil himself is there.'

Then it was Jergli's turn to speak,

> 'If it be not, it's at least his mother,
> Or else it's the Devil's own step-brother.'

And now Marli had a bright thought, and said to Veitli,

> 'Advance, Veitli, advance, advance,
> And I behind will hold the lance.'

Veitli, however, did not attend to that, and Jackli said,

> ''Tis Schulz's place the first to be,
> No one deserves that honor but he.'

Then Master Schulz plucked up his courage, and said, gravely,

> 'Then let us boldly advance to the fight,
> And thus we shall show our valour and might.'

Hereupon, they all together set on the dragon. Master Schulz crossed himself and prayed for God's assistance, but as all this was of no avail, and he was getting nearer and nearer to the enemy, he screamed 'Oho! oho! ho! ho! ho!' in the greatest anguish. This awakened the hare, which in great alarm darted swiftly away. When Master Schulz saw her thus flying from the field of battle, he cried in his joy.

'Quick, Veitli, quick, look there, look there,
The monster's nothing but a hare!'

But the Swabian allies went in search of further adventures, and came to the Moselle, a mossy, quiet, deep river, over which there are few bridges, and which in many places people have to cross in boats. As the seven Swabians did not know this, they called to a man who was working on the opposite side of the river, to know how people contrived to get across. The distance and their way of speaking made the man unable to understand what they wanted, and he said, 'What? what?' in the way people speak in the neighborhood of Treves.

Master Schulz thought he was saying, 'Wade, wade through the water,' and as he was the first, began to set out and went into the Moselle. It was not long before he sank in the mud and the deep waves which drove against him, but his hat was blown on the opposite shore by the wind, and a frog sat down beside it, and croaked, 'Wat, wat, wat.'

The other six on the opposite side heard that, and said, 'Oho, comrades, Master Schulz is calling us; if he can wade across, why cannot we?' So they all jumped into the water together in a great hurry, and were drowned, and thus one frog took the lives of all six of them, and not one of the Swabian allies ever reached home again.

THE DEVIL AND HIS GRANDMOTHER

There was a great war, and the King had many soldiers, but gave them small pay, so small that they could not live upon it, so three of them agreed among themselves to desert. One of them said to the others, 'If we are caught, we shall be hanged on the gallows; how shall we manage it?' Another said, 'Look at that great cornfield, if we were to hide ourselves there, no one could find us; the troops are not allowed to enter it, and tomorrow they are to march away.'

They crept into the corn, only the troops did not march away, but remained lying all round about it. They stayed in the corn for two days and two nights, and were so hungry that they all but died, but if they had come out, their death would have been certain. Then said they, 'What is the use of our deserting if we have to perish miserably here?' But now a fiery dragon came flying through the air, and it came down to them, and asked why they had concealed themselves there? They answered, 'We are three soldiers who have deserted because the pay was so bad, and now we shall have to die of hunger if we stay here, or to dangle on the gallows if we go out.'

'If you will serve me for seven years,' said the dragon, 'I will convey you through the army so that no one shall seize you.'

'We have no choice and are compelled to accept,' they replied. Then the dragon caught hold of them with his claws, and carried them away through the air over the army, and put them down again on the earth far from it; but the dragon was no other than the Devil. He gave them a small whip and said, 'Whip with it and crack it, and then as much gold will spring up round about as you can wish for; then you can live like great lords, keep horses, and drive your carriages, but when the seven years have come to an end, you are my property.' Then he put before them a book which they were all three forced to sign.

'I will, however, then set you a riddle,' said he, 'and if you can guess that, you shall be free, and released from my power.'

Then the dragon flew away from them, and they went away with their whip, had gold in plenty, ordered themselves rich apparel and travelled about the world.

Wherever they were, they lived in pleasure and magnificence, rode on horseback, drove in carriages, ate and drank, but did nothing wicked. The time slipped quickly away, and when the seven years were coming to an end, two of them were terribly anxious and alarmed; but the third took the affair easily, and said, 'Brothers, fear nothing, my head is sharp enough, I shall guess the riddle.'

They went out into the open country and sat down, and the two pulled sorrowful faces. Then an aged woman came up to them who inquired why they were so sad? 'Alas!' said they, 'how can that concern you? After all, you cannot help us.'

'Who knows?' said she. 'Confide your trouble to me.'

So they told her that they had been the Devil's servants for nearly seven years, and that he had provided them with gold as plentifully as if it had been blackberries, but that they had sold themselves to him, and were forfeited to him, if at the end of the seven years they could not guess a riddle.

The old woman said, 'If you are to be saved, one of you must go into the forest. There he will come to a fallen rock which looks like a little house. He must enter that, and then he will obtain help.'

The two melancholy ones thought to themselves, 'That will still not save us,' and stayed where they were, but the third, the merry one, got up and walked on in the forest until he found the rock house. In the little house, however, a very aged woman was sitting, who was the Devil's grandmother, and asked the soldier where he came from, and what he wanted there? He told her everything that had happened, and as he pleased her well, she had pity on him, and said she would help him. She lifted up a great stone, which lay above a cellar, and said, 'Conceal thyself there, thou canst hear everything that is said here; only sit still, and do not stir. When the dragon comes, I will question him about the riddle, he tells everything to me, so listen carefully to his answer.'

At twelve o'clock at night, the dragon came flying thither, and asked for his dinner. The grandmother laid the table, and served up food and drink, so that he was pleased, and they ate and drank together. In the course of conversation, she asked him what kind of a day he had had, and how many souls he had got?

'Nothing went very well today,' he answered, 'but I have laid hold of three soldiers, I have them safe.'

'Indeed! three soldiers, that's something like, but they may escape you yet.'

The Devil said mockingly, 'They are mine! I will set them a riddle, which they will never in this world be able to guess!'

'What riddle is that?' she inquired.

'I will tell you. In the great North Sea lies a dead dogfish, that shall be your roast meat, and the rib of a whale shall be your silver spoon, and a hollow old horse's hoof shall be your wineglass.'

When the Devil had gone to bed, the old grandmother raised

up the stone, and let out the soldier. 'Hast thou paid particular attention to everything?'

'Yes,' said he, 'I know enough, and will contrive to save myself.' Then he had to go back another way, through the window, secretly and with all speed to his companions. He told them how the Devil had been overreached by the old grandmother, and how he had learned the answer to the riddle from him. Then they were all joyous, and of good cheer, and took the whip and whipped so much gold for themselves that it ran all over the ground.

When the seven years had fully gone by, the Devil came with the book, showed the signatures, and said, 'I will take you with me to hell. There you shall have a meal! If you can guess what kind of roast meat you will have to eat, you shall be free and released from your bargain, and may keep the whip as well.'

Then the first soldier began and said, 'In the great North Sea lies a dead dogfish, that no doubt is the roast meat.'

The Devil was angry, and began to mutter, 'Hm! hm! hm!' And asked the second, 'But what will your spoon be?'

'The rib of a whale, that is to be our silver spoon.'

The Devil made a wry face, again growled, 'Hm! hm! hm!' and said to the third, 'And do you also know what your wineglass is to be?'

'An old horse's hoof is to be our wineglass.'

Then the Devil flew away with a loud cry, and had no more power over them, but the three kept the whip, whipped as much money for themselves with it as they wanted, and lived happily to their end.

THE IRON STOVE

In the days when wishing was still of some use, a King's son was bewitched by an old witch, and shut up in an iron stove in a forest. There he passed many years, and no one could deliver him. Then a King's daughter came into the forest, who had lost herself, and could not find her father's kingdom again. After she had wandered about for nine days, she at length came to the iron stove. Then a voice came forth from it, and asked her, 'Whence comest thou, and whither goest, thou?' She answered, 'I have lost my father's kingdom, and cannot get home again.' Then a voice inside the iron stove said, 'I will help thee to get home again, and that indeed most swiftly, if thou wilt promise to do what I desire of thee. I am the son of a far greater King than thy father, and I will marry thee.'

Then was she afraid, and thought, 'Good heavens! What can I do with an iron stove?' But as she much wished to get home to her father, she promised to do as he desired. But he said, 'Thou shalt return here, and bring a knife with thee, and scrape a hole in the iron.' Then he gave her a companion who walked near her, but did not speak, but in two hours he took her home; there was great joy in the castle when the King's daughter came home, and the old King fell on her neck and kissed her.

She, however, was sorely troubled, and said, 'Dear father, what I have suffered! I should never have got home again from the great wild forest, if I had not come to an iron stove, but I have been forced to give my word that I will go back to it, set it free, and marry it.'

Then the old King was so terrified that he all but fainted, for he had but this one daughter. They therefore resolved that they would send, in her place, the miller's daughter, who was very beautiful. They took her there, gave her a knife, and said she was to scrape at the iron stove. So she scraped at it for four-and-twenty hours, but could not bring off the least morsel of it. When day dawned, a voice in the stove said, 'It seems to me it is day outside.' Then she answered, 'It seems so to me too; I fancy I hear the noise of my father's mill.'

'So thou art a miller's daughter! Then go thy way at once, and let the King's daughter come here.'

Then she went away at once, and told the old King that the man outside there, would have none of her – he wanted the King's daughter. They, however, still had a swine-herd's daughter, who was even prettier than the miller's daughter, and they determined to give her a piece of gold to go to the iron stove instead of the King's daughter. So she was taken thither, and she also had to scrape for four-and-twenty hours. She, however, made nothing of it.

When day broke, a voice inside the stove cried, 'It seems to me it is day outside!' Then answered she, 'So it seems to me also; I fancy I hear my father's horn blowing.'

'Then thou art a swine-herd's daughter! Go away at once, and tell the King's daughter to come, and tell her all must be done as promised, and if she does not come, everything in the kingdom shall be ruined and destroyed, and not one stone be left standing on another.'

When the King's daughter heard that she began to weep, but

now there was nothing for it but to keep her promise. So she took leave of her father, put a knife in her pocket, and went forth to the iron stove in the forest. When she got there, she began to scrape, and the iron gave way, and when two hours were over, she had already scraped a small hole. Then she peeped in, and saw a youth so handsome, and so brilliant with gold and with precious jewels, that her very soul was delighted. Now, therefore, she went on scraping, and made the hole so large that he was able to get out. Then said he, 'Thou art mine, and I am thine; thou art my bride, and hast released me.'

He wanted to take her away with him to his kingdom, but she entreated him to let her go once again to her father, and the King's son allowed her to do so, but she was not to say more to her father than three words, and then she was to come back again. So she went home, but she spoke more than three words, and instantly the iron stove disappeared, and was taken far away over glass mountains and piercing swords; but the King's son was set free, and no longer shut up in it.

After this she bade goodbye to her father, took some money with her, but not much, and went back to the great forest, and looked for the iron stove, but it was nowhere to be found. For nine days she sought it, and then her hunger grew so great that she did not know what to do, for she could no longer live. When it was evening, she seated herself in a small tree, and made up her mind to spend the night there, as she was afraid of wild beasts. When midnight drew near, she saw in the distance a small light, and thought, 'Ah, there I should be saved!' She got down from the tree, and went towards the light, but on the way she prayed. Then she came to a little old house, and much grass had grown all about it, and a small heap of wood lay in front of it. She

THE IRON STOVE

thought, 'Ah, whither have I come,' and peeped in through the window, but she saw nothing inside but toads, big and little, except a table well covered with wine and roast meat, and the plates and glasses were of silver. Then she took courage, and knocked at the door. The fat toad cried,

> 'Little green waiting-maid,
> Waiting-maid with the limping leg,
> Little dog of the limping leg,
> Hop hither and thither,
> And quickly see who is without.'

And a small toad came walking by and opened the door to her. When she entered, they all bade her welcome, and she was forced to sit down. They asked, 'Where hast thou come from, and whither art thou going?'

Then she related all that had befallen her, and how because she had transgressed the order which had been given her not to say more than three words, the stove, and the King's son also, had disappeared, and now she was about to seek him over hill and dale until she found him. Then the old fat one said,

> 'Little green waiting-maid,
> Waiting-maid with the limping leg,
> Little dog of the limping leg,
> Hop hither and thither,
> And bring me the great box.'

Then the little one went and brought the box. After this they gave her meat and drink, and took her to a well-made bed, which felt like silk and velvet, and she laid herself therein, in God's name, and slept. When morning came she arose, and the old toad gave her three needles out of the great box which she was to take with her; they would be needed by her, for she had to cross a high, glass mountain, and go over three piercing swords and a great lake. If she did all this, she would get her lover back again. Then she gave her three things, which she was to take the greatest care of, namely, three large needles, a plough-wheel, and three nuts.

With these she travelled onwards, and when she came to the glass mountain which was so slippery, she stuck the three needles first behind her feet and then before them, and so got over it, and when she was over it, she hid them in a place which she marked carefully. After this, she came to the three piercing swords, and then she seated herself on her plough-wheel, and rolled over them.

At last, she arrived in front of a great lake, and when she had crossed it, she came to a large and beautiful castle. She went and asked for a place; she was a poor girl, she said, and would like to be hired. She knew, however, that the King's son whom she had released from the iron stove in the great forest was in the castle. Then she was taken on as a scullery-maid at low wages. But, already the King's son had another maiden by his side whom he wanted to marry, for he thought that she had long been dead.

In the evening, when she had washed up and was done, she felt in her pocket and found the three nuts which the old toad had given her. She cracked one with her teeth, and was going to eat the kernel when lo and behold there was a stately royal garment in it! But when the bride heard of this she came and asked for the dress, and wanted to buy it, and said, 'It is not a dress for a servant-girl.' But she said no, she would not sell it, but if the bride would grant her one thing she should have it, and that was, leave to sleep one night in her bridegroom's chamber. The bride gave her permission because the dress was so pretty, and she had never had one like it. When it was evening she said to her bridegroom, 'That silly girl will sleep in thy room.'

'If thou art willing so am I,' said he. She, however, gave him a glass of wine in which she had poured a sleeping draught. So the bridegroom and the scullery-maid went to sleep in the room, and he slept so soundly that she could not waken him.

She wept the whole night and cried, 'I set thee free when thou wert in an iron stove in the wild forest, I sought thee, and walked over a glass mountain, and three sharp swords, and a great lake before I found thee, and yet thou wilt not hear me!'

The servants sat by the chamber door, and heard how she thus wept the whole night through, and in the morning they told it to their lord.

And the next evening when she had washed up, she opened the second nut, and a far more beautiful dress was within it, and when the bride beheld it, she wished to buy that also. But the girl would not take money, and begged that she might once again sleep in the bridegroom's chamber. The bride, however, gave him a sleeping drink, and he slept so soundly that he could hear nothing. But the scullery maid wept the whole night long, and cried, 'I set thee free when thou wert in an iron stove in the wild forest, I sought thee, and walked over a glass mountain, and over three sharp swords and a great lake before I found thee, and yet thou wilt not hear me!'

The servants sat by the chamber door and heard her weeping the whole night through, and in the morning informed their lord of it. And on the third evening, when she had washed up, she opened the third nut, and within it was a still more beautiful dress which was stiff with pure gold. When the bride saw that she wanted to have it, but the maiden only gave it up on condition that she might for the third time sleep in the bridegroom's apartment.

The King's son was, however, on his guard, and threw the sleeping draught away. Now, therefore, when she began to weep and to cry, 'Dearest love, I set thee free when thou wert in the iron stove in the terrible wild forest,' the King's son leapt up and said, 'Thou art the true one, thou art mine, and I am thine.'

Thereupon, while it was still night, he got into a carriage with her, and they took away the false bride's clothes so that she could not get up. When they came to the great lake, they sailed across it, and when they reached the three sharp-cutting swords they seated themselves on the plough-wheel, and when they got to the glass mountain they thrust the three needles in it, and so at length they got to the little old house; but when they went inside that, it was a great castle, and the toads were all disenchanted, and were King's children, and full of happiness. Then the wedding was celebrated, and the King's son and the princess remained in the castle, which was much larger than the castles of their fathers. As, however, the old King grieved at being left alone, they fetched him away, and brought him to live with them, and they had two kingdoms, and lived in happy wedlock.

A mouse did run,
This story is done.

THE LAZY SPINNER

In a certain village there once lived a man and his wife, and the wife was so idle that she would never work at anything; whatever her husband gave her to spin, she did not get done, and what she did spin she did not wind, but let it all remain entangled in a heap. If the man scolded her, she was always ready with her tongue, and said, 'Well, how should I wind it, when I have no reel? Just you go into the forest and get me one.'

'If that is all,' said the man, 'then I will go into the forest, and get some wood for making reels.'

Then the woman was afraid that if he had the wood he would make her a reel of it, and she would have to wind her yarn off, and then begin to spin again. She bethought herself a little, and then a lucky idea occurred to her, and she secretly followed the man into the forest, and when he had climbed into a tree to choose and cut the wood, she crept into the thicket below where he could not see her, and cried,

'He who cuts wood for reels shall die,
And he who winds, shall perish.'

The man listened, laid down his axe for a moment, and began to consider what that could mean. 'Hello,' he said at last, 'what can that have been; my ears must have been singing, I won't alarm myself for nothing.' So he again seized the axe, and began to hew, then again there came a cry from below:

'He who cuts wood for reels shall die,
And he who winds, shall perish.'

He stopped, and felt afraid and alarmed, and pondered over the circumstance. But when a few moments had passed, he took heart again, and a third time he stretched out his hand for the axe, and began to cut. But some one called out a third time, and said loudly,

'He who cuts wood for reels shall die,
And he who winds, shall perish.'

That was enough for him, and all inclination had departed from him, so he hastily descended the tree, and set out on his way home.

The woman ran as fast as she could by by-ways so as to get home first. So when he entered the parlour, she put on an innocent look as if nothing had happened, and said, 'Well, have you brought a nice piece of wood for reels?'

'No,' said he, 'I see very well that winding won't do,' and told her what had happened to him in the forest, and from that time forth left her in peace about it.

Nevertheless after some time, the man again began to complain of the disorder in the house. 'Wife,' said he, 'it is really a shame that the spun yarn should lie there all entangled!'

'I'll tell you what,' said she, 'as we still don't come by any reel, go you up into the loft, and I will stand down below, and will throw the yarn up to you, and you will throw it down to me, and so we shall get a skein after all.'

'Yes, that will do,' said the man. So they did that, and when it was done, he said, 'The yarn is in skeins, now it must be boiled.' The woman was again distressed; she certainly said, 'Yes, we will boil it next morning early.' But she was secretly contriving another trick.

Early in the morning she got up, lit a fire, and put the kettle on, only instead of the yarn, she put in a lump of tow, and let it boil. After that she went to the man who was still lying in bed, and said to him, 'I must just go out, you must get up and look after the yarn which is in the kettle on the fire, but you must be at hand at once; mind that, for if the cock should happen to crow, and you are not attending to the yarn, it will become tow.'

The man was willing and took good care not to loiter. He got up as quickly as he could, and went into the kitchen. But when he reached the kettle and peeped in, he saw, to his horror, nothing but a lump of tow. Then the poor man was as still as a mouse, thinking he had neglected it, and was to blame, and in future said no more about yarn and spinning.

But you yourself must own she was an odious woman!

THE FOUR SKILFUL BROTHERS

There was once a poor man who had four sons, and when they were grown up, he said to them, 'My dear children, you must now go out into the world, for I have nothing to give you, so set out, and go to some distance and learn a trade, and see how you can make your way.'

So the four brothers took their sticks, bade their father farewell, and went through the town gate together. When they had travelled about for some time, they came to a crossroads which branched off in four different directions. Then said the eldest, 'Here we must separate, but on this day four years, we will meet each other again at this spot, and in the meantime we will seek our fortunes.'

Then each of them went his way, and the eldest met a man who asked him where he was going, and what he was intending to do? 'I want to learn a trade,' he replied. Then the other said, 'Come with me, and be a thief.'

'No,' he answered, 'that is no longer regarded as a reputable trade, and the end of it is that one has to swing on the gallows.'

'Oh,' said the man, 'you need not be afraid of the gallows; I will only teach you to get such things as no other man could ever lay hold of, and no one will ever detect you.'

So he allowed himself to be talked into it, and while with the man became an accomplished thief, and so dexterous that nothing was safe from him, if he once desired to have it.

The second brother met a man who put the same question to

him about what he wanted to learn in the world. 'I don't know yet,' he replied.

'Then come with me, and be an astronomer; there is nothing better than that, for nothing is hid from you.'

He liked the idea, and became such a skilful astronomer that when he had learnt everything, and was about to travel onwards, his master gave him a telescope and said to him, 'With that you canst thou see whatsoever takes place either on earth or in heaven, and nothing can remain concealed from thee.'

A huntsman took the third brother into training, and gave him such excellent instruction in everything that related to huntsmanship, that he became an experienced hunter. When he went away, his master gave him a gun and said, 'It will never fail you; whatsoever you aim at, you are certain to hit.'

The youngest brother also met a man who spoke to him, and inquired what his intentions were. 'Would you not like to be a tailor?' said he.

'Not that I know of,' said the youth; 'sitting doubled up from morning till night, driving the needle and the goose backwards and forwards, is not to my taste.'

'Oh, but you are speaking in ignorance,' answered the man; 'with me you would learn a very different kind of tailoring, which is respectable and proper, and for the most part very honorable.'

So he let himself be persuaded, and went with the man, and learnt his art from the very beginning. When they parted, the man gave the youth a needle, and said, 'With this you can sew together whatever is given you, whether it is as soft as an egg or as hard as steel; and it will all become one piece of stuff, so that no seam will be visible.'

When the appointed four years were over, the four brothers

arrived at the same time at the crossroads, embraced and kissed each other, and returned home to their father.

'So now,' said he, quite delighted, 'the wind has blown you back again to me.'

They told him of all that had happened to them, and that each had learnt his own trade. Now they were sitting just in front of the house under a large tree, and the father said, 'I will put you all to the test, and see what you can do.' Then he looked up and said to his second son, 'Between two branches up at the top of this tree, there is a chaffinch's nest, tell me how many eggs there are in it?'

The astronomer took his glass, looked up, and said, 'There are five.'

Then the father said to the eldest, 'Fetch the eggs down without disturbing the bird which is sitting hatching them.'

The skilful thief climbed up, and took the five eggs from beneath the bird, which never observed what he was doing, and remained quietly sitting where she was, and brought them down to his father. The father took them, and put one of them on each corner of the table, and the fifth in the middle, and said to the huntsman, 'With one shot thou shalt shoot me the five eggs in two, through the middle.'

The huntsman aimed, and shot the eggs, all five as the father had desired, and that at one shot. He certainly must have had some of the powder for shooting round corners.

'Now it's your turn,' said the father to the fourth son; 'you shall sew the eggs together again, and the young birds that are inside them as well, and you must do it so that they are not hurt by the shot.'

The tailor brought his needle, and sewed them as his father

wished. When he had done this the thief had to climb up the tree again, and carry them to the nest, and put them back again under the bird without her being aware of it. The bird sat her full time, and after a few days the young ones crept out, and they had a red line round their necks where they had been sewn together by the tailor.

'Well,' said the old man to his sons, 'I begin to think you are worth more than green clover; you have used your time well, and learnt something good. I can't say which of you deserves the most praise. That will be proved if you have but an early opportunity of using your talents.'

Not long after this, there was a great uproar in the country, for the King's daughter was carried off by a dragon. The King was full of trouble about it, both by day and night, and caused it to be proclaimed that whosoever brought her back should have her to wife. The four brothers said to each other, 'This would be a fine opportunity for us to show what we can do!' and resolved to go forth together and liberate the King's daughter.

'I will soon know where she is,' said the astronomer, and looked through his telescope and said, 'I see her already, she is far away from here on a rock in the sea, and the dragon is beside her watching her.' Then he went to the King, and asked for a ship for himself and his brothers, and sailed with them over the sea until they came to the rock.

There the King's daughter was sitting, and the dragon was lying asleep on her lap. The huntsman said, 'I dare not fire, I should kill the beautiful maiden at the same time.'

'Then I will try my art,' said the thief, and he crept thither and stole her away from under the dragon, so quietly and dexterously, that the monster never remarked it, but went on snoring. Full of joy, they hurried off with her on board ship, and steered out into the open sea; but the dragon, who when he awoke had found no princess there, followed them, and came snorting angrily through the air. Just as he was circling above the ship, and about to descend on it, the huntsman shouldered his gun, and shot him to the heart. The monster fell down dead, but was so large and powerful that his fall shattered the whole ship.

Fortunately, however, they laid hold of a couple of planks, and swam about the wide sea. Then again they were in great peril, but the tailor, who was not idle, took his wondrous needle, and with a few stitches sewed the planks together, and they seated themselves upon them, and collected together all the fragments of the vessel. Then he sewed these so skilfully together, that in a very short time the ship was once more seaworthy, and they could go home again in safety.

When the King once more saw his daughter, there were great rejoicings. He said to the four brothers, 'One of you shall have her to wife, but which of you it is to be you must settle among yourselves.'

Then a warm contest arose among them, for each of them preferred his own claim. The astronomer said, 'If I had not seen the princess, all your arts would have been useless, so she is mine.'

The thief said, 'What would have been the use of your seeing, if I had not got her away from the dragon? So she is mine.'

The huntsman said, 'You and the princess, and all of you, would have been torn to pieces by the dragon if my ball had not hit him, so she is mine.'

The tailor said, 'And if I, by my art, had not sewn the ship together again, you would all of you have been miserably drowned, so she is mine.'

Then the King uttered this saying, 'Each of you has an equal right, and as all of you cannot have the maiden, none of you shall have her, but I will give to each of you, as a reward, half a kingdom.'

The brothers were pleased with this decision, and said, 'It is better thus than that we should be at variance with each other.' Then each of them received half a kingdom, and they lived with their father in the greatest happiness as long as it pleased God.

THE LAMBKIN AND THE LITTLE FISH

There were once a little brother and a little sister, who loved each other with all their hearts. Their own mother was, however, dead, and they had a step-mother, who was not kind to them, and secretly did everything she could to hurt them. It so happened that the two were playing with other children in a meadow before the house, and there was a pond in the meadow which came up to one side of the house. The children ran about it, and caught each other, and played at counting out.

'Eneke Beneke, let me live,
And I to thee my bird will give.
The little bird, it straw shall seek,
The straw I'll give to the cow to eat.
The pretty cow shall give me milk,
The milk I'll to the baker take.
The baker he shall bake a cake,
The cake I'll give unto the cat.
The cat shall catch some mice for that,
The mice I'll hang up in the smoke,
And then you'll see the snow.'

They stood in a circle while they played this, and the one to whom the word 'snow' fell, had to run away and all the others ran after him and caught him. As they were running about so merrily the step-mother watched them from the window, and grew angry. And as she understood arts of witchcraft she bewitched them both, and changed the little brother into a fish, and the little sister into a lamb. Then the fish swam here and there about the pond and was very sad, and the lambkin walked up and down the meadow, and was miserable, and could not eat or touch one blade of grass.

Thus passed a long time, and then strangers came as visitors to the castle. The false step-mother thought, 'This is a good opportunity,' and called the cook and said to him, 'Go and fetch the lamb from the meadow and kill it, we have nothing else for the visitors.' Then the cook went away and got the lamb, and took it into the kitchen and tied its feet, and all this it bore patiently. When he had drawn out his knife and was whetting it on the doorstep to kill the lamb, he noticed a little fish swimming backwards and forwards in the water, in front of the kitchen-sink and looking up at him. This, however, was the brother, for when the fish saw the cook take the lamb away, it followed them and swam along the pond to the house; then the lamb cried down to it,

'Ah, brother, in the pond so deep,
How sad is my poor heart!
Even now the cook he whets his knife
To take away my tender life.'

The little fish answered,

'Ah, little sister, up on high
How sad is my poor heart
While in this pond I lie.'

When the cook heard that the lambkin could speak and said such sad words to the fish down below, he was terrified and thought this could be no common lamb, but must be bewitched by the wicked woman in the house. Then said he, 'Be easy, I will not kill thee,' and took another sheep and made it ready for the guests, and conveyed the lambkin to a good peasant woman, to whom he related all that he had seen and heard.

The peasant was, however, the very woman who had been foster-mother to the little sister, and she suspected at once who the lamb was, and went with it to a wise woman. Then the wise woman pronounced a blessing over the lambkin and the little fish, by means of which they regained their human forms, and after this she took them both into a little hut in a great forest, where they lived alone, but were contented and happy.

THE OLD MAN MADE YOUNG AGAIN

In the time when our Lord still walked this earth, he and St Peter stopped one evening at a smith's and received free quarters. Then it came to pass that a poor beggar, hardly pressed by age and infirmity, came to this house and begged alms of the smith. St Peter had compassion on him and said, 'Lord and master, if it please thee, cure his torments that he may be able to win his own bread.'

The Lord said kindly, 'Smith, lend me thy forge, and put on some coals for me, and then I will make this ailing old man young again.' The smith was quite willing, and St Peter blew the bellows, and when the coal fire sparkled up large and high our Lord took the little old man, pushed him in the forge in the midst of the red-hot fire, so that he glowed like a rose-bush, and praised God with a loud voice.

After that the Lord went to the quenching tub, put the glowing little man into it so that the water closed over him, and after he had carefully cooled him, gave him his blessing, when behold the little man sprang nimbly out, looking fresh, straight, healthy, and as if he were but twenty. The smith, who had watched everything closely and attentively, invited them all to supper. He, however, had an old half-blind crooked, mother-in-law who went to the youth, and with great earnestness asked if the fire had burnt him much. He answered that he had never felt more comfortable, and that he had sat in the red heat as if he had been in cool dew. The youth's words echoed in the ears of the old woman all night long, and early next morning, when the Lord had gone on his way again and had heartily thanked the smith, the latter thought he might make his old mother-in-law young again likewise, as he had watched everything so carefully, and it lay in the province of his trade. So he called to ask her if she, too, would like to go bounding about like a girl of eighteen. She said, 'With all my heart, as the youth has come out of it so well.'

So the smith made a great fire, and thrust the old woman into it, and she writhed about this way and that, and uttered terrible cries of murder.

'Sit still; why art thou screaming and jumping about so?' cried he, and as he spoke he blew the bellows again until all her rags were burnt. The old woman cried without ceasing, and the smith thought to himself, 'I have not quite the right art,' and took her out and threw her into the cooling-tub.

Then she screamed so loudly that the smith's wife upstairs and her daughter-in-law heard, and they both ran downstairs, and saw the old woman lying in a heap in the quenching-tub, howling and screaming, with her face wrinkled and shrivelled and all out of shape. Thereupon the two, who were both with child, were so terrified that that very night two boys were born who were not made like men but apes, and they ran into the woods, and from them sprang the race of apes.

SNOW-WHITE AND ROSE-RED

There was once a poor widow who lived in a lonely cottage. In front of the cottage was a garden wherein stood two rose-trees, one of which bore white and the other red roses. She had two children who were like the two rose-trees, and one was called Snow-White, and the other Rose-Red. They were as good and happy, as busy and cheerful as ever two children in the world were, only Snow-White was more quiet and gentle than Rose-Red. Rose-Red liked better to run about in the meadows and fields seeking flowers and catching butterflies; but Snow-White sat at home with her mother, and helped her with her housework, or read to her when there was nothing to do.

The two children were so fond of each another that they always held each other by the hand when they went out together, and when Snow-White said, 'We will not leave each other,' Rose-Red answered, 'Never so long as we live,' and their mother would add, 'What one has she must share with the other.'

They often ran about the forest alone and gathered red berries, and no beasts did them any harm, but came close to them trustfully. The little hare would eat a cabbage-leaf out of their hands, the roe grazed by their side, the stag leapt merrily by them, and the birds sat still upon the boughs, and sang whatever they knew.

No mishap overtook them; if they had stayed too late in the forest, and night came on, they laid themselves down near one another upon the moss, and slept until morning came, and their mother knew this and had no distress on their account.

Once when they had spent the night in the wood and the dawn had roused them, they saw a beautiful child in a shining white dress sitting near their bed. He got up and looked quite kindly at them, but said nothing and went away into the forest. And when they looked round they found that they had been sleeping quite close to a precipice, and would certainly have fallen into it in the darkness if they had gone only a few paces further. And their mother told them that it must have been the angel who watches over good children.

Snow-White and Rose-Red kept their mother's little cottage so neat that it was a pleasure to look inside it. In the summer Rose-Red took care of the house, and every morning laid a wreath of flowers by her mother's bed before she awoke, in which was a rose from each tree. In the winter Snow-White lit the fire and hung the kettle on the wrekin. The kettle was of copper and shone like gold, so brightly was it polished. In the evening, when the snowflakes fell, the mother said, 'Go, Snow-White, and bolt the door,' and then they sat round the hearth, and the mother took her spectacles and read aloud out of a large book, and the two girls listened as they sat and span. And close by them lay a lamb upon the floor, and behind them upon a perch sat a white dove with its head hidden beneath its wings.

One evening, as they were thus sitting comfortably together, someone knocked at the door as if he wished to be let in. The mother said, 'Quick, Rose-Red, open the door, it must be a traveller who is seeking shelter.' Rose-Red went and pushed back the bolt, thinking that it was a poor man, but it was not; it was a bear that stretched his broad, black head within the door.

Rose-Red screamed and sprang back, the lamb bleated, the dove fluttered, and Snow-White hid herself behind her mother's bed. But the bear began to speak and said, 'Do not be afraid, I will do you no harm! I am half-frozen, and only want to warm myself a little beside you.'

'Poor bear,' said the mother, 'lie down by the fire, only take care that you do not burn your coat.' Then she cried, 'Snow-White, Rose-Red, come out, the bear will do you no harm, he means well.' So they both came out, and by and by the lamb and dove came nearer, and were not afraid of him. The bear said, 'Here, children, knock the snow out of my coat a little.' So they brought the broom and swept the bear's hide clean; and he stretched himself by the fire and growled contentedly and comfortably. It was not long before they grew quite at home, and played tricks with their clumsy guest. They tugged his hair with their hands, put their feet upon his back and rolled him about, or they took a hazel-switch and beat him, and when he growled they laughed. But the bear took it all in good part, only when they were too rough he called out,

'Leave me alive, children,
"Snowy-White, Rosy-Red,
Will you beat your lover dead?"'

When it was bedtime, and the others went to bed, the mother said to the bear, 'You can lie there by the hearth, and then you will be safe from the cold and the bad weather.' As soon as day dawned the two children let him out, and he trotted across the snow into the forest.

Henceforth, the bear came every evening at the same time, laid himself down by the hearth, and let the children amuse themselves with him as much as they liked; and they got so used to him that the doors were never fastened until their black friend had arrived.

When spring had come and all outside was green, the bear said one morning to Snow-White, 'Now I must go away, and cannot come back for the whole summer.'

'Where are you going, then, dear bear?' asked Snow-White.

'I must go into the forest and guard my treasures from the wicked dwarfs. In the winter, when the earth is frozen hard, they are obliged to stay below and cannot work their way through; but now, when the sun has thawed and warmed the earth, they break through it, and come out to pry and steal; and what once gets into their hands, and in their caves, does not easily see daylight again.'

Snow-White was quite sorry for his going away, and as she unbolted the door for him, and the bear was hurrying out, he caught against the bolt and a piece of his hairy coat was torn off, and it seemed to Snow-White as if she had seen gold shining through it, but she was not sure about it. The bear ran away quickly, and was soon out of sight behind the trees.

A short time afterwards the mother sent her children into the forest to get firewood. There they found a big tree which lay felled on the ground, and close by the trunk something was jumping backwards and forwards in the grass, but they could not make out what it was. When they came nearer they saw a dwarf with an old withered face and a snow-white beard a yard long. The end of the beard was caught in a crevice of the tree, and the little fellow was jumping backwards and forwards like a dog tied to a rope, and did not know what to do.

He glared at the girls with his fiery red eyes and cried, 'Why do you stand there? Can you not come here and help me?'

'What are you about there, little man?' asked Rose-Red.

'You stupid, prying goose!' answered the dwarf; 'I was going to split the tree to get a little wood for cooking. The little bit of food that one of us wants gets burnt up directly with thick logs; we do not swallow so much as you coarse, greedy folk. I had just driven the wedge safely in, and everything was going as I wished; but the wretched wood was too smooth and suddenly sprang asunder, and the tree closed so quickly that I could not pull out my beautiful white beard; so now it is tight in and I cannot get away, and the silly, sleek, milk-faced things laugh! Ugh! how odious you are!'

The children tried very hard, but they could not pull the beard out, it was caught too fast. 'I will run and fetch someone,' said Rose-Red.

'You senseless goose!' snarled the dwarf; 'why should you fetch somone? You are already two too many for me; can you not think of something better?'

'Don't be impatient,' said Snow-White, 'I will help you,' and she pulled her scissors out of her pocket, and cut off the end of the beard.

As soon as the dwarf felt himself free he laid hold of a bag which lay amongst the roots of the tree, and which was full of gold, and lifted it up, grumbling to himself, 'Uncouth people, to cut off a piece of my fine beard. Bad luck to you!' and then he swung the bag upon his back, and went off without even once looking at the children.

Some time after that Snow-White and Rose-Red went to catch a dish of fish. As they came near the brook they saw something like a large grasshopper jumping towards the water, as if it were going to leap in. They ran to it and found it was the dwarf. 'Where are you going?' said Rose-Red; 'you surely don't want to go into the water?'

'I am not such a fool!' cried the dwarf; 'don't you see that the accursed fish wants to pull me in?' The little man had been sitting there fishing, and unluckily the wind had twisted his beard with the fishing-line; just then a big fish bit, and the feeble creature had not strength to pull it out; the fish kept the upper hand and pulled the dwarf towards him. He held on to all the reeds and rushes, but it was of little good, he was forced to follow the movements of the fish, and was in urgent danger of being dragged into the water.

The girls came just in time; they held him fast and tried to free his beard from the line, but all in vain, beard and line were entangled fast together. Nothing was left but to bring out the scissors and cut the beard, whereby a small part of it was lost. When the dwarf saw that he screamed out, 'Is that civil, you toadstool, to disfigure one's face? Was it not enough to clip off the end of my beard? Now you have cut off the best part of it. I cannot let myself be seen by my people. I wish you had been made to run the soles off your shoes!' Then he took out a sack of pearls which lay in the rushes, and without saying a word more he dragged it away and disappeared behind a stone.

It happened that soon afterwards the mother sent the two children to the town to buy needles and thread, and laces and ribbons. The road led them across a heath upon which huge pieces of rock lay strewn here and there. Now they noticed a large bird hovering in the air, flying slowly round and round above them; it sank lower and lower, and at last settled near a rock not far off. Directly afterwards they heard a loud, piteous cry. They ran up and saw with horror that the eagle had seized their old acquaintance the dwarf, and was going to carry him off.

The children, full of pity, at once took tight hold of the little man, and pulled against the eagle so long that at last he let his booty go. As soon as the dwarf had recovered from his first fright he cried with his shrill voice, 'Could you not have done it more carefully! You dragged at my brown coat so that it is all torn and full of holes, you helpless clumsy creatures!' Then he took up a sack full of precious stones, and slipped away again under the rock into his hole. The girls, who by this time were used to his thanklessness, went on their way and did their business in the town.

As they crossed the heath again on their way home, they surprised the dwarf, who had emptied out his bag of precious stones in a clean spot, and had not thought that anyone would come there so late. The evening sun shone upon the brilliant stones; they glittered and sparkled with all colours so beautifully that the children stood still and looked at them. 'Why do you stand gaping there?' cried the dwarf, and his ashen-grey face became copper-red with rage. He was going on with his bad words when a loud growling was heard, and a black bear came trotting towards them out of the forest. The dwarf sprang up in a fright, but he could not get to his cave, for the bear was already close. Then in the dread of his heart he cried, 'Dear Mr Bear, spare me, I will give you all my treasures; look, the beautiful jewels lying there! Grant me my life; what do you want with such a slender little fellow as I? You would not feel me between your teeth. Come, take these two wicked girls, they are tender morsels for you, fat as young quails; for mercy's sake eat them!' The bear took no heed of his words, but gave the wicked creature a single blow with his paw, and he did not move again.

The girls had run away, but the bear called to them, 'Snow-White and Rose-Red, do not be afraid; wait, I will come with you.' Then they knew his voice and waited, and when he came up to them suddenly his bearskin fell off, and he stood there, a handsome man, clothed all in gold. 'I am a King's son,' he said, 'and I was bewitched by that wicked dwarf, who had stolen my treasures; I have had to run about the forest as a savage bear until I was freed by his death. Now he has got his well-deserved punishment.'

Snow-White was married to him, and Rose-Red to his brother, and they divided between them the great treasure, which the dwarf had gathered together in his cave. The old mother lived peacefully and happily with her children for many years. She took the two rose-trees with her, and they stood before her window, and every year bore the most beautiful roses, white and red.

THE DURATION OF LIFE

When God had created the world and was about to fix the length of each creature's life, the ass came and asked, 'Lord, how long shall I live?'

'Thirty years,' replied God; 'does that content thee?'

'Ah, Lord,' answered the ass, 'that is a long time. Think of my painful existence! To carry heavy burdens from morning to night, to drag sacks of corn to the mill, that others may eat bread, to be cheered and refreshed with nothing but blows and kicks. Relieve me of a portion of this long time.'

Then God had pity on him and relieved him of eighteen years. The ass went away comforted, and the dog appeared. 'How long wouldst thou like to live?' said God to him. 'Thirty years are too many for the ass, but thou wilt be satisfied with that.'

'Lord,' answered the dog, 'is that thy will? Consider how I shall have to run, my feet will never hold out so long, and when I have once lost my voice for barking, and my teeth for biting, what will be left for me to do but run from one corner to another and growl?'

God saw that he was right, and released him from twelve years of life. Then came the monkey. 'Thou wilt certainly live thirty years willingly?' said the Lord to him. 'Thou hast no need to work as the ass and the dog have to do, and wilt always enjoy thyself.'

'Ah! Lord,' he answered, 'it may seem as if that were the case, but it is quite different. When it rains porridge I have no spoon.

I am always to play merry pranks, and make faces which force people to laugh, and if they give me an apple, and I bite into it, why it is sour! How often sadness hides itself behind mirth! I shall never be able to hold out for thirty years.' God was gracious and took off ten.

At last man appeared, joyous, healthy and vigorous, and begged God to appoint his time for him. 'Thirty years shalt thou live,' said the Lord. 'Is that enough for thee?' 'What a short time,' cried man, 'when I have built my house and my fire burns on my own hearth; when I have planted trees which blossom and bear fruit, and am just intending to enjoy my life, I am to die! O Lord, lengthen my time.'

'I will add to it the ass's eighteen years,' said God.

'That is not enough,' replied the man.

'Thou shalt also have the dog's twelve years.'

'Still too little!'

'Well, then,' said God, 'I will give thee the monkey's ten years also, but more thou shalt not have.' The man went away, but was not satisfied.

So man lives seventy years. The first thirty are his human years, which are soon gone; then is he healthy, merry, works with pleasure, and is glad of his life. Then follow the ass's eighteen years, when one burden after another is laid on him, he has to carry the corn which feeds others, and blows and kicks are the reward of his faithful services. Then come the dog's twelve years, when he lies in the corner, and growls and has no longer any teeth to bite with, and when this time is over the monkey's ten years form the end. Then man is weak-headed and foolish, does silly things, and becomes the jest of the children.

DEATH'S MESSENGERS

In ancient times a giant was once travelling on a great highway, when suddenly an unknown man sprang up before him, and said, 'Halt, not one step farther!'

'What!' cried the giant, 'a creature whom I can crush between my fingers, wants to block my way? Who art thou that thou darest to speak so boldly?'

'I am Death,' answered the other. 'No one resists me, and thou also must obey my commands.'

But the giant refused, and began to struggle with Death. It was a long, violent battle. At last the giant got the upper hand, and struck Death down with his fist, so that he dropped by a stone. The giant went his way, and Death lay there conquered, and so weak that he could not get up again. 'What will be done now,' said he, 'if I stay lying here in a corner? No one will die in the world, and it will get so full of people that they won't have room to stand beside each other.'

In the meantime a young man came along the road, who was strong and healthy, singing a song, and glancing around on every side. When he saw the half-fainting one, he went compassionately to him, raised him up, poured a strengthening draught out of his flask for him, and waited till he came round.

'Dost thou know,' said the stranger, whilst he was getting up, 'who I am, and who it is whom thou hast helped on his legs again?'

'No,' answered the youth, 'I do not know thee.'

'I am Death,' said he. 'I spare no one, and can make no exception with thee, but that thou mayst see that I am grateful, I promise thee that I will not fall on thee unexpectedly, but will send my messengers to thee before I come and take thee away.'

'Well,' said the youth, 'it is something gained that I shall know when thou comest, and at any rate be safe from thee for so long.' Then he went on his way, and was light-hearted, and enjoyed himself, and lived without thought. But youth and health did not last long, soon came sicknesses and sorrows, which tormented him by day, and took away his rest by night. 'Die, I shall not,' said he to himself, 'for Death will send his messengers before that, but I do wish these wretched days of sickness were over.'

As soon as he felt himself well again he began once more to live merrily. Then one day someone tapped him on the shoulder. He looked round, and Death stood behind him, and said, 'Follow me, the hour of thy departure from this world has come.'

'What,' replied the man, 'wilt thou break thy word? Didst thou not promise me that thou wouldst send thy messengers to me before coming thyself? I have seen none!'

'Silence!' answered Death. 'Have I not sent one messenger to thee after another? Did not fever come and smite thee, and shake thee, and cast thee down? Has dizziness not bewildered thy head? Has not gout twitched thee in all thy limbs? Did not thine ears sing? Did not toothache bite into thy cheeks? Was it not dark before thine eyes? And besides all that, has not my own brother Sleep reminded thee every night of me? Didst thou not lie by night as if thou wert already dead?'

The man could make no answer; he yielded to his fate, and went away with Death.

THE HARE AND THE HEDGEHOG

This story, my dear young folks, seems to be false, but it really is true, for my grandfather, from whom I have it, used always, when relating it, to say complacently, 'It must be true, my son, or else no one could tell it to you.' The story is as follows.

One Sunday morning, about harvest time, just as the buckwheat was in bloom, the sun was shining brightly in heaven, the east wind was blowing warmly over the stubble-fields, the larks were singing in the air, the bees buzzing among the buckwheat, the people were all going in their Sunday clothes to church, and all creatures were happy, and the hedgehog was happy, too.

The hedgehog, however, was standing by his door with his arms akimbo, enjoying the morning breezes, and slowly trilling a little song to himself, which was neither better nor worse than the songs which hedgehogs are in the habit of singing on a blessed Sunday morning. Whilst he was thus singing half aloud to himself, it suddenly occurred to him that, while his wife was washing and drying the children, he might very well take a walk into the field, and see how his turnips were going on. The turnips were, in fact, close beside his house, and he and his family were accustomed to eat them, for which reason he looked upon them as his own. No sooner said than done. The hedgehog shut the house door behind him, and took the path to the field. He had not gone very far from home, and was just turning round the sloe-bush which stands there outside the field, to go up into the turnip-field, when he observed the hare who had gone out on business of the same kind, namely, to visit his cabbages. When the hedgehog caught sight of the hare, he bade him a friendly good morning. But the hare, who was in his own way a distinguished gentleman, and frightfully haughty, did not return the hedgehog's greeting, but said to him, assuming at the same time a very contemptuous manner, 'How do you happen to be running about here in the field so early in the morning?'

'I am taking a walk,' said the hedgehog.

'A walk!' said the hare, with a smile. 'It seems to me that you might use your legs for a better purpose.'

This answer made the hedgehog furiously angry, for he can bear anything but an attack on his legs, just because they are crooked by nature. So now the hedgehog said to the hare, 'You seem to imagine that you can do more with your legs than I with mine.'

'That is just what I do think,' said the hare.

'That can be put to the test,' said the hedgehog. 'I wager that if we run a race, I will outstrip you.'

'That is ridiculous! You with your short legs!' said the hare, 'but for my part I am willing, if you have such a monstrous fancy for it. What shall we wager?'

'A golden louis-d'or and a bottle of brandy,' said the hedgehog.

'Done,' said the hare. 'Shake hands on it, and then we may as well come off at once.'

'Nay,' said the hedgehog, 'there is no such great hurry! I am still fasting, I will go home first, and have a little breakfast. In half-an-hour I will be back again at this place.'

Hereupon the hedgehog departed, for the hare was quite satisfied with this. On his way the hedgehog thought to himself,

'The hare relies on his long legs, but I will contrive to get the better of him. He may be a great man, but he is a very silly fellow, and he shall pay for what he has said.' So when the hedgehog reached home, he said to his wife, 'Wife, dress thyself quickly, thou must go out to the field with me.'

'What is going on, then?' said his wife.

'I have made a wager with the hare, for a gold louis-d'or and a bottle of brandy. I am to run a race with him, and thou must be present.'

'Good heavens, husband,' the wife now cried, 'art thou not right in thy mind, hast thou completely lost thy wits? What can make thee want to run a race with the hare?'

'Hold thy tongue, woman,' said the hedgehog, 'that is my affair. Don't begin to discuss things which are matters for men. Be off, dress thyself, and come with me.' What could the hedgehog's wife do? She was forced to obey him, whether she liked it or not.

So when they had set out on their way together, the hedgehog said to his wife, 'Now pay attention to what I am going to say. Look you, I will make the long field our race-course. The hare shall run in one furrow, and I in another, and we will begin to run from the top. Now all that thou hast to do is to place thyself here below in the furrow, and when the hare arrives at the end of the furrow, on the other side of thee, thou must cry out to him, "I am here already!"'

Then they reached the field, and the hedgehog showed his wife her place, and then walked up the field. When he reached the top, the hare was already there. 'Shall we start?' said the hare.

'Certainly,' said the hedgehog. 'Then both at once.'

So saying, each placed himself in his own furrow. The hare counted, 'Once, twice, thrice, and away!' and went off like a whirlwind down the field. The hedgehog, however, only ran about three paces, and then he stooped down in the furrow, and stayed quietly where he was. When the hare therefore arrived in full career at the lower end of the field, the hedgehog's wife met him with the cry, 'I am here already!'

The hare was shocked and wondered not a little. He thought no other than that it was the hedgehog himself who was calling to him, for the hedgehog's wife looked just like her husband. The hare, however, thought to himself, 'That has not been done fairly,' and cried, 'It must be run again, let us have it again.' And once more he went off like the wind in a storm, so that he seemed to fly. But the hedgehog's wife stayed quietly in her place. So when the hare reached the top of the field, the hedgehog himself cried out to him, 'I am here already.'

The hare, however, quite beside himself with anger, cried, 'It must be run again, we must have it again.'

'All right,' answered the hedgehog, 'for my part we'll run as often as you choose.' So the hare ran seventy-three times more, and the hedgehog always held out against him, and every time the hare reached either the top or the bottom, either the hedgehog or his wife said, 'I am here already.'

At the seventy-fourth time, however, the hare could no longer reach the end. In the middle of the field he fell to the ground, blood streamed out of his mouth, and he lay dead on the spot. But the hedgehog took the louis-d'or which he had won and the bottle of brandy, called his wife out of the furrow, and both went home together in great delight, and if they are not dead, they are living there still.

This is how it happened that the hedgehog made the hare run races with him on the Buxtehuder[1] heath till he died, and since

---

[1] Buxtehuder is a village near Hamburg

that time no hare has ever had any fancy for running races with a Buxtehuder hedgehog.

The moral of this story, however, is, firstly, that no one, however great he may be, should permit himself to jest at any one beneath him, even if he be only a hedgehog. And, secondly, it teaches, that when a man marries, he should take a wife in his own position, who looks just as he himself looks. So whosoever is a hedgehog let him see to it that his wife is a hedgehog also, and so forth.

THE CRYSTAL BALL

There was once an enchantress, who had three sons who loved each other as brothers, but the old woman did not trust them, and thought they wanted to steal her power from her. So she changed the eldest into an eagle, which was forced to dwell in the rocky mountains, and was often seen sweeping in great circles in the sky. The second, she changed into a whale, which lived in the deep sea, and all that was seen of it was that it sometimes spouted up a great jet of water in the air. Each of them only bore his human form for two hours daily. The third son, who was afraid she might change him into a raging wild beast – a bear perhaps, or a wolf – went secretly away.

He had heard that a King's daughter who was bewitched, was imprisoned in the Castle of the Golden Sun, and was waiting for deliverance. Those, however, who tried to free her risked their lives; three-and-twenty youths had already died a miserable death, and now only one other might make the attempt, after which no more must come. And as his heart was without fear, he caught at the idea of seeking out the Castle of the Golden Sun. He had already travelled about for a long time without being able to find it, when he came by chance into a great forest, and did not know the way out of it. All at once he saw in the distance two giants, who made a sign to him with their hands, and when he came to them they said, 'We are quarrelling about a cap, and which of us it is to belong to, and as we are equally strong, neither of us can get the better of the other. The small men are cleverer than we are, so we will leave the decision to thee.'

'How can you dispute about an old cap?' said the youth.

'Thou dost not know what properties it has! It is a wishing-cap; whosoever puts it on, can wish himself away wherever he likes, and in an instant he will be there.'

'Give me the cap,' said the youth, 'I will go a short distance off, and when I call you, you must run a race, and the cap shall belong to the one who gets first to me.'

He put it on and went away, and thought of the King's daughter, forgot the giants, and walked continually onward. At length he sighed from the very bottom of his heart, and cried, 'Ah, if I were but at the Castle of the Golden Sun,' and hardly had the words passed his lips than he was standing on a high mountain before the gate of the castle.

He entered and went through all the rooms, until in the last he found the King's daughter. But how shocked he was when he saw her. She had an ashen-grey face full of wrinkles, bleary eyes, and red hair. 'Are you the King's daughter, whose beauty the whole world praises?' cried he.

'Ah,' she answered, 'this is not my form; human eyes can only see me in this state of ugliness, but that thou mayst know what I am like, look in the mirror. It does not let itself be misled, it will show thee my image as it is in truth.' She gave him the mirror in his hand, and he saw therein the likeness of the most beautiful maiden on earth, and saw, too, how the tears were rolling down her cheeks with grief.

Then said he, 'How canst thou be set free? I fear no danger.'

She said, 'He who gets the crystal ball, and holds it before the enchanter, will destroy his power with it, and I shall resume my true shape. Ah,' she added, 'so many have already gone to meet death for this, and thou art so young; I grieve that thou shouldst encounter such great danger.'

'Nothing can keep me from doing it,' said he, 'but tell me what I must do.'

'Thou shalt know everything,' said the King's daughter; 'when thou descendest the mountain on which the castle stands, a wild bull will stand below by a spring, and thou must fight with it, and if thou hast the luck to kill it, a fiery bird will spring out of it, which bears in its body a burning egg, and in the egg the crystal ball lies like a yolk. The bird will not, however, let the egg fall until forced to do so, and if it falls on the ground, it will flame up and burn everything that is near, and melt even ice itself, and with it the crystal ball, and then all thy trouble will have been in vain.'

The youth went down to the spring, where the bull snorted and bellowed at him. After a long struggle he plunged his sword in the animal's body, and it fell down. Instantly, a fiery bird arose from it, and was about to fly away, but the young man's brother, the eagle, who was passing between the clouds, swooped down, hunted it away to the sea, and struck it with his beak until, in its extremity, it let the egg fall.

The egg did not, however, fall into the sea, but on a fisherman's hut which stood on the shore and the hut began at once to smoke and was about to break out in flames. Then arose in the sea waves as high as a house, they streamed over the hut, and subdued the fire. The other brother, the whale, had come swimming to them, and had driven the water up on high. When the fire was extinguished, the youth sought for the egg and happily found it; it was not yet melted, but the shell was broken by being so suddenly cooled with the water, and he could take out the crystal ball unhurt.

When the youth went to the enchanter and held it before him, the latter said, 'My power is destroyed, and from this time forth thou art the King of the Castle of the Golden Sun. With this canst thou likewise give back to thy brothers their human form.'

Then the youth hastened to the King's daughter, and when he entered the room, she was standing there in the full splendour of her beauty, and joyfully they exchanged rings with each other.

THE BOOTS OF BUFFALO-LEATHER

A soldier who is afraid of nothing, troubles himself about nothing. One of this kind had received his discharge, and as he had learnt no trade and could earn nothing, he travelled about and begged alms of kind people. He had an old waterproof on his back, and a pair of riding-boots of buffalo leather, which were still left to him.

One day, he was walking he knew not where, straight out into the open country, and at length came to a forest. He did not know where he was, but saw sitting on the trunk of a tree, which had been cut down, a man who was well dressed and wore a green shooting-coat. The soldier shook hands with him, sat down on the grass by his side, and stretched out his legs. 'I see thou hast good boots on, which are well blacked,' said he to the huntsman; 'but if thou hadst to travel about as I have, they would not last long. Look at mine, they are of buffalo leather, and have been worn for a long time, but in them I can go through thick and thin.' After a while the soldier got up and said, 'I can stay no longer, hunger drives me onwards; but, Brother Bright-boots, where does this road lead to?'

'I don't know that myself,' answered the huntsman, 'I have lost my way in the forest.'

'Then thou art in the same plight as I,' said the soldier; 'birds of a feather flock together, let us remain together, and seek our way.'

The huntsman smiled a little, and they walked on further and further, until night fell. 'We do not get out of the forest,' said the soldier, 'but there in the distance I see a light shining, which will help us to something to eat.'

They found a stone house, knocked at the door, and an old woman opened it. 'We are looking for quarters for the night,' said the soldier, 'and some lining for our stomachs, for mine is as empty as an old knapsack.'

'You cannot stay here,' answered the old woman; 'this is a robber's house, and you would do wisely to get away before they come home, or you will be lost.'

'It won't be so bad as that,' answered the soldier, 'I have not had a mouthful for two days, and whether I am murdered here or die of hunger in the forest is all the same to me. I shall go in.'

The huntsman would not follow, but the soldier drew him in with him by the sleeve. 'Come, my dear brother, we shall not come to an end so quickly as that!'

The old woman had pity on them and said, 'Creep in here behind the stove, and if they leave anything, I will give it to you on the sly when they are asleep.'

Scarcely were they in the corner before twelve robbers came bursting in, seated themselves at the table which was already laid, and vehemently demanded some food. The old woman brought in some great dishes of roast meat, and the robbers enjoyed that thoroughly.

When the smell of the food ascended the nostrils of the soldier, he said to the huntsman, 'I cannot hold out any longer, I shall seat myself at the table, and eat with them.'

'Thou wilt bring us to destruction,' said the huntsman, and held him back by the arm. But the soldier began to cough loudly. When the robbers heard that, they threw away their knives and forks, leapt up, and discovered the two who were behind the stove. 'Aha, gentlemen, are you in the corner?' cried they, 'What are you doing here? Have you been sent as spies? Wait a while, and you shall learn how to fly on a dry bough.'

'But do be civil,' said the soldier, 'I am hungry, give me something to eat, and then you can do what you like with me.' The robbers were astonished, and the captain said, 'I see that thou hast no fear; well, thou shalt have some food, but after that thou must die.'

'We shall see,' said the soldier, and seated himself at the table, and began to cut away valiantly at the roast meat. 'Brother Brightboots, come and eat,' cried he to the huntsman; 'thou must be as hungry as I am, and cannot have better roast meat at home,' but the huntsman would not eat.

The robbers looked at the soldier in astonishment, and said, 'The rascal uses no ceremony.' After a while he said, 'I have had enough food, now get me something good to drink.' The captain was in the mood to humour him in this also, and called to the old woman, 'Bring a bottle out of the cellar, and mind it be of the best.' The soldier drew the cork out with a loud noise, and then went with the bottle to the huntsman and said, 'Pay attention, brother, and thou shalt see something that will surprise thee; I am now going to drink the health of the whole clan.'

Then he brandished the bottle over the heads of the robbers, and cried, 'Long life to you all, but with your mouths open and your right hands lifted up,' and then he drank a hearty draught. Scarcely were the words said than they all sat motionless as if made of stone, and their mouths were open and their right hands stretched up in the air. The huntsman said to the soldier, 'I see that thou art acquainted with tricks of another kind, but now come and let us go home.'

'Oho, my dear brother, but that would be marching away far too soon; we have conquered the enemy, and must first take the booty. Those men there are sitting fast, and are opening their mouths with astonishment, but they will not be allowed to move until I permit them. Come, eat and drink.'

The old woman had to bring another bottle of the best wine, and the soldier would not stir until he had eaten enough to last for three days. At last when day came, he said, 'Now it is time to strike our tents, and that our march may be a short one, the old woman shall show us the nearest way to the town.'

When they had arrived there, he went to his old comrades, and said, 'Out in the forest I have found a nest full of gallows' birds. Come with me and we will take it.'

The soldier led them, and said to the huntsman, 'Thou must go back again with me to see how they shake when we seize them by the feet.' He placed the men round about the robbers, and then he took the bottle, drank a mouthful, brandished it above them, and cried, 'Live again.' Instantly, they all regained the power of movement, but were thrown down and bound hand and foot with cords. Then the soldier ordered them to be thrown into a cart as if they had been so many sacks, and said, 'Now drive them straight to prison.'

The huntsman, however, took one of the men aside and gave him another commission besides.

'Brother Bright-boots,' said the soldier, 'we have safely routed the enemy and been well fed, now we will quietly walk behind them as if we were stragglers!' When they approached the town, the soldier saw a crowd of people pouring through the gate of the town, who were raising loud cries of joy, and waving green boughs in the air. Then he saw that the entire bodyguard was coming up.

'What can this mean?' said he to the huntsman.

'Dost thou not know?' he replied, 'that the King has for a long time been absent from his kingdom, and that today he is returning, and everyone is going to meet him.'

'But where is the King?' said the soldier, 'I do not see him.'

'Here he is,' answered the huntsman, 'I am the King, and have announced my arrival.'

Then he opened his hunting coat, and his royal garments were visible. The soldier was alarmed, and fell on his knees and begged him to forgive him for having in his ignorance treated him as an equal, and spoken to him by such a name. But the King shook hands with him, and said, 'Thou art a brave soldier, and hast saved my life. Thou shalt never again be in want, I will take care of thee. And if ever thou wouldst like to eat a piece of roast meat, as good as that in the robber's house, come to the royal kitchen. But if thou wouldst drink a health, thou must first ask my permission.'

THE GOLDEN KEY

In the wintertime, when deep snow lay on the ground, a poor boy was forced to go out on a sledge to fetch wood. When he had gathered it together, and packed it, he wished, as he was so frozen with cold, not to go home at once, but to light a fire and warm himself a little.

So he scraped away the snow, and as he was thus clearing the ground, he found a tiny, gold key. Hereupon, he thought that where the key was, the lock must be also, and dug in the ground and found an iron chest. 'If the key does but fit it!' thought he; 'no doubt there are precious things in that little box.'

He searched, but no keyhole was there. At last he discovered one, but so small that it was hardly visible. He tried it, and the key fitted it exactly. Then he turned it once round, and now we must wait until he has quite unlocked it and opened the lid, and then we shall learn what wonderful things were lying in that box.